ShopTalk

Shop Talk

Lessons in Teaching from an African American Hair Salon

Yolanda J. Majors

Foreword by Carol D. Lee

TEACHERS COLLEGE PRESS

TEACHERS COLLEGE | COLUMBIA UNIVERSITY

NEW YORK AND LONDON

Published by Teachers College Press, 1234 Amsterdam Avenue, New York, NY 10027

Photo and photo artwork appearing in Figures 1.1 and 2.1 courtesy of Raphael Nash.

Portions of Chapter 4 appeared in "Shoptalk: Teaching and Learning in an African American Hair Salon," Yolanda J. Majors, *Mind, Culture, and Activity, 10*(4), 289–310, reprinted by permission of Taylor and Francis LLC (http://www.tandfonline.com).

Portions of Chapter 8 appeared in Y. Majors, J. Kim, and S. Ansari, "Beyond Hip-Hop: A Cultural Context View of Literacy." In L. Christenbury, J. Bomer, and P. Smagorinsky (Eds.), *Handbook of Adolescent Literacy Research.* Copyright 2009, Copyright Guilford Press. Reprinted with permission of the Guilford Press.

Library of Congress Cataloging-in-Publication Data is available at loc.gov

Majors, Yolanda J.
    Shoptalk : lessons in teaching from an African American hair salon / Yolanda J. Majors ; foreword by Carol D. Lee.
      pages cm
    Includes bibliographical references and index.
    ISBN 978-0-8077-5661-4 (pbk.)—ISBN 978-0-8077-5662-1 (case)—ISBN 978-0-8077-7383-3 (ebook)
      1. Teaching—Anecdotes. 2. Beauty shops—Social aspects. 3. Hairdressing of African Americans. 4. African American women. I. Title.
    LB1027.M3162 2015
    371.102—dc23

                                                            2015012458

ISBN 978-0-8077-5661-4 (paper)
ISBN 978-0-8077-5662-1 (hardcover)
ISBN 978-0-8077-7383-3 (ebook)

Contents

Foreword

In *Shoptalk*, Yolanda Majors joins the path breaking work of Shirley Brice Heath (1983) (uses of narrative in low income African American and European American households), Marjorie Goodwin (1990) (problem solving and negotiations of power as African American and Latino/a American children play street games) and Mike Rose (2004) (problem solving and identity wrestling on the factory floor). She enters spaces that are off the academic radar screen, presumed to be only ordinary, presumed not to be spaces of rigorous problem solving, spaces to which we are blind in considering where and how people of various ages, through their participation in everyday activity, engage intellective dispositions to use Gordon's (Gordon & Bridglall, 2006) term and problem solving that under appropriate circumstances have the power to propel meaningful movement across different sites of intellective work.

Majors joins the ranks of scholars who examine the cognitive processes and social interactions that support problem solving in everyday contexts that display heuristic connections to problem solving in academic disciplines. She contributes to the building of a powerful research methodology: bridging cognition, disciplinary problem solving, sociolinguistics, critical discourse analysis, human development foci on identity development and motivation, and the political lens of critical race theory—no small feat. A breadth bespeaking a renaissance scholar, not siloed in a single discipline or a single conceptual framework.

Why is this investigation into the social and intellectual ecology of the African American hair salon important? Majors is concerned with the ubiquitous inequalities in opportunity to learn, particularly with regard to school based literacies, among young people who are positioned negatively with regard to perceptions of them as racialized beings, presumed to be locked as with a naturalized destiny inside the bowels of poverty, with vulnerabilities often exacerbated by racialized perceptions of gender. Our society creates institutional ecologies that reify these positionings, that reinforce these positionings, and in fact create these positionings. At the publication of this book, we see the unfolding of these inequities on the streets of Ferguson, Missouri, New York City, Sanford, Florida, Columbus, Ohio, Charleston,

South Carolina, and Baltimore, Maryland, where unarmed Black boys and men have been shot by police and communities within these cities, across the nation and indeed the world have protested and raised questions about underlying conditions of racism and poverty that have contributed to these tragedies.

Shoptalk pushes against the often unstated but implied and widely accepted public assumptions that people who are negatively positioned with regard to assumptions about race and poverty are only victims, are pawns, as having no agency unless "saved" by some outside other. She demonstrates in the stories of *Shoptalk* how ordinary people, across the life course, interrogate the politics, the ideologies, the economics with which they must wrestle everyday. And perhaps most importantly, how through the meditational powers of structured ways of talking, employing the tools and dialogical meaning making processes entailed in what Smitherman (1977, 2000) calls the African American English Rhetorical Tradition, participants are invited and supported in taking on multiple points of view, critical self-reflection, close textual analyses, and complex problem solving.

Why is the question of the affordances of what Majors calls *Shoptalk* important as a potential tool to support what she calls border crossing? In this book, Majors examines and illustrates how the features and fundamental guiding principles of Shoptalk offer a framework for expanding opportunities for participation, engagement, and complex problem solving in classrooms. While she argues for its relevance in Language Arts classrooms, I would argue that the broader framework is not limited to Language Arts, but is important for engagement and participation in classrooms focusing on other academic domains as well. In the context of schooling, the Shoptalk framework asserts that classrooms must be socializing spaces, spaces in which all participants feel safe to be assertive, to be vulnerable because in falling they are supported, to take on and wrestle with perspectives with which they may not initially agree, and to be supported in making personally meaningful connections with the problems and content of learning. The wise scholar Edmund Gordon (Gordon & Bridglall, 2006) calls these intellective dispositions, which learners can draw upon as they attempt to navigate across diverse spaces of problem solving, a vision of schooling that goes beyond the acquisition of academic content. If such intellective border crossing requires what Gutiérrez and Rogoff (2003) call expansive repertoires of practice, then clearly the practices and framing of Shoptalk provide guidance.

What Majors illustrates in the classroom examples of bringing Shoptalk into the classroom is another powerful big idea about teaching and learning. That is, what facilitates transfer of repertoires from one field of practice to another is the degree to which the new site of practice takes into account, scaffolds and extends the repertoires that novices, new learners bring with them. It is precisely this conceptualization of dialogic pathways through which we move within and across spaces that marks robust learning environments. It is a fundamental precept of learning that is not only about working toward social justice ends for those who are disenfranchised along so many dimensions, but is a foundational principle of learning that applies regardless of who are the students. Thus the challenge is to expand our understandings of how the intellective dispositions that Majors describes are socialized across different settings, with different players, toward an array of learning goals. Without question, Majors has made a significant contribution to the development of the field of education's repertory of exemplars of robust learning environments.

Carol D. Lee, Ph.D.
Edwina S. Tarry Professor of Education and Social Policy
Northwestern University

REFERENCES

Goodwin, M. (1990). *He-said-she-said: Talk as social organization.* Bloomington, IN: Indiana University Press.

Gordon, E.W., & Bridglall, B.L. (Eds.). (2006). *The affirmative development of academic abilities.* Boulder, CO: Rowman and Littlefield Publishers.

Gutierrez, K., & Rogoff, B. (2003). Cultural ways of learning: Individual traits or repertoires of practice. *Educational Researcher, 32*(5), 19–25.

Heath, S.B. (1983). *Ways with words: Language, life and work in communities and classrooms.* New York, NY: Cambridge University Press.

Rose, M. (2004). *The mind at work: Valuing the intelligence of the American worker.* New York, NY: Penguin.

Smitherman, G. (1977). *Talkin' and testifyin': The language of black america.* Boston, MA: Houghton Mifflin.

Smitherman, G. (2000). *Talk that talk: Language, culture and education in African America.* New York, NY: Routledge.

Acknowledgments

This book would not have happened without the insights, guidance, and encouragement of many people too numerous to list by name, but who each contributed in special ways. I am indebted to the men and women of the hair salons who graciously opened their businesses, hearts, and minds to me, while patiently answering my questions under the scrutiny of video cameras and audio recorders. A special thanks to the Chambers, Jackson, Bellamy, and Hall-Staples families. The participating school, principals, department chairs, and teachers tilled, fertilized, and cultivated the vision of community talk in the classroom. For their time, patience, and partnership I am indebted to Christopher Kelly, Barry McRaith, Robert Karpenski, Senita Murphy, Stephanie Adess Bell, and Yvette Vessel. This book is as much their harvest as it is mine.

Shoptalk: Lessons in Teaching from an African American Hair Salon began in an Iowa beauty salon. This book and my own scholarly development benefited tremendously from the support, inspiration, and feedback of many who taught and encouraged me to question and believe. Carol D. Lee, my friend and mentor, claimed and nourished me through my graduate program and inspired this work through her research on Cultural Modeling. Bonnie Sunstein helped set the stage early in my career by shaping my skills in ethnographic observation. Cynthia Lewis and Cathy Roller both stimulated my interest in literacy and offered perspective and invaluable feedback on my work. Finally, James D. Marshall challenged me to dig deep and dance through the pouring ambiguity until the sun shone. Thank you, Jim, for always holding the umbrella over me. Their combined insight helped me to create a book that I wanted to write—and still feel to be important.

I have been blessed throughout my life to have encountered people whose talents and grace are greater than my own. The writing of this book and the ideas therein are products of their wisdom and generosity. A special thanks to Donna Alvermann, Bill Ayers, Arnetha Ball, Phil Bowman, Shirley Brice-Heath, Courtney Cazden, Michael Cole, Fred Erickson, Judith Green, Kris Gutierrez, George Hillocks, Barbara Rogoff, Mike Rose, Peter Smagorinsky, and James V. Wertsch for intellectual nourishment as this project slowly grew. I am also grateful to have had the generous support of the Spencer Foundation and contributions from the National Council of Teachers of English, Holmes Scholars Foundation, University of Georgia, University of Illinois at Chicago, and the Minnesota Center for Reading Research—each of which provided me with the financial resources and institutional supports to study, research, and write. To Jean Ward, Lori Tate, and the incredible editors and staff of Teachers College Press, who shared my enthusiasm and helped fine-tune the vision behind this book, this could not have happened without you.

I would especially like to thank Hsiu-Ting Hung, Ernise Singleton, Ritu Radhakrishnan, and Kate Anderson for their contributions to the research of the hair salons; Sana Ansari, Hongmei Dong, Jung E. Kim, Danielle A. Smith, Lasana Kazembe, Duane Davis, and Astrid Suarez for their collaborations, critiques, curriculum design support, and creative eyes; and Shannon Dahmes, Annie Ittner, Lori Laster, Kay Rosheim, and Jamie Kreil for their amazing research assistance, editorial suggestions, and belief in this project. It is their collective hands, eyes, and hearts that guided the work of this book at various stages. Thanks to Shona Burke and Meaghan L. Tongen for eagle-eyed copyediting and constructive feedback; and to all of the students with whom I've worked in both the university and high school who provided me with constant inspiration and the reason to move forward.

To each of these individuals, I offer my deepest thanks. Although this project would not have seen the light of day without them, the support of friends and family tethered me and kept me moving forward. I thank the Madhubuti-Lee family, Baba Haki and Mama Safisha for their unyielding love and support; the Wimberly, Caldwell, Sanders, and Nash families for building what can be neither broken nor dulled; Nailah Suad Nasir, Tryphenia Peele-Eady, and Kimberly Dawn Clark for being the steel that sharpens steel. I thank my children, Myles, Christen, and Olivia, for being resilient and modeling for me that which I wish to become someday; my incredible mother, Phyllis K. Nash, and my brothers Martice and Raphael Nash, whose unyielding love inspires every dream I've ever held; and Stephanie to whom I dedicate this book as a gift for being gifts and strength to me. Finally, for his unfaltering ability to love deeply, patiently and unconditionally, to see clearly, to listen with integrity and speak with insight, I offer my deepest gratitude and heartfelt thanks to my husband, Christopher Jon Majors.

Introduction

Literacy is a socially organized, ideological, and situated practice that is implicated in power relations and embedded with specific cultural meanings, traditions, and norms (Barton, Hamilton, & Ivanic, 2003; Luke, 2003; Scribner & Cole, 1981), and so too is talk in the hair salon. To be literate, some suggest, is to display skill in decoding both written and oral texts (Resnick & Resnick, 1977)—texts that are intimately bound to the particular details and nuances of people's everyday lives and the varied cultural ways they make sense of those details (Scribner & Cole, 1981). Such skill, like that involved in literary interpretation, comprises institutional and cultural technology—the hammers and nails of social, ideological, and goal-directed practice (Lee, 2007). As a kind of practice, one that involves "recurrent, goal-directed sequence of activities using a particular technology and particular system of knowledge," literacy is "not simply knowing how to decode particular scripts, but applying this knowledge for specific purposes in specific contexts of use" (Scribner & Cole, 1981 p. 236). The skills of literacy, it follows then, are cultivated in particular social, cultural, and linguistic contexts, within and across spaces and time, classrooms being one space of many (Cole, 1996). Take, for example, the following exchange, which took place during one of my visits to a local, community hair salon.

"You know the reason that Black people could be slaves is because they could stand the heat!" Slowly taking a seat beneath the whirring, stationary hair dryer, Ms. Addie[1] smooths the creases of her red and white chambray checkered hoop skirt, while Wendi, her beautician, checks the heat setting and lowers the hood, before motioning for her next client, Ms. Fields, to take a seat in the chair at her station.

"You right about that," replies Ms. Fields with a nod. "Hell, we know we can stand some heat, as much as they 'den gave us!"

As laughter erupts, Ms. Addie pokes her head out from beneath the buzzing dryer as if to say something, but slowly shakes her head and decides against it upon catching the stern eye of Wendi as she applies a white cream to sections of Ms. Fields's shortened, gray hair.

"You'd be surprised by how many of us schoolteachers don't know how to deal with our own history," Ms. Addie says loudly from beneath the dryer, earning Wendi's approving nod. "So this month, I decided that for each day of Black History Month, I would dress up and become someone famous in our history and teach my 2nd-graders by pretending to be a famous person from our past."

Dressed as Miss Harriet Tubman, the African American abolitionist, humanitarian, and Union spy/soldier who led enslaved men, women, and children into northern U.S. free states and Canada, Ms. Addie points downward and directs our gaze to a wiggling set of legs showing off knee-length, mismatched wool socks and a worn and tattered pair of black military boots. Around her neck dangles a thick link chain with a rusted shackle attached at one end.

"These boots are my husband's," she continues. "My students love it, though. They say, 'Ms. Addie, who are you today?' And I tell 'em, 'My name is Harriet Tubman. I am a slave and the reason I have stockings that are different colors is because as a slave we were only given one set of clothes a year.'"

"Uhm! Girl, that's deep!" Ms. Fields responds, furrowing her brows and slowly shaking her head.

"Yes!" Ms. Addie continues, "and I say to them if they want to tell me something, they have to call me by the name of that person. So like when the principal came in, he asked the class, 'Well, who is she today?' And the students said, 'Oh, she's Miss Tubman.' And so he asked, 'Well, where is Ms. Addie?' And the kids said, 'Oh, she's got a cold.'"

After a brief pause, the salon erupts once more in laughter. Ms. Addie continues, "And each day during the month I show up as somebody different. You should have seen me as George Washington Carver. Folks at the bank thought I was crazy."

A collective frown and verbal pause fill the room and let me know that folks were imagining, if not questioning, what it must have been like to bump into either of these heroes while in line at the grocery store.

"Now, I know you didn't go out in the street like that?" asks Ms. Fields.

"I sure did! I went to the grocery store! I went to the bank! I even went to Home Depot!" Ms. Addie states. Proudly lifting her chest and pulling her head away from the dryer, she continues, "But you know the surprising thing is how the grown folks react and the other teachers that I work with. They don't like it, you know they whisper and all."

Eyebrows raised, Ms. Addie throws me a "You know what I'm talking about" nod, then retreats under the dryer.

This book, in part, is about how people, like Ms. Addie, talk to one another in the African American hair salon. It documents the encounters they share, the identities they resist and create, the literate skills they display in doing so, and the lessons learned from their collective and complex social readings of the world. It is about talk as performative discourse, where clients, beauticians, and other community members act out skillful, culturally scripted roles for their and others' benefit (Duranti, 1997; Gee, 1997; Goffman, 1969). Together, these "social actors" (Goffman, 1981) effortlessly and deliberately take center stage, circulating a counter-discourse in a well-rehearsed effort to "formulate oppositional interpretations of their identities, interests, and needs" (Fraser, 1989, p. 123). To do so, however, requires skill, competence, and know-how—like that involved in the kind of literary interpretation typically ascribed to academics—including the ability to draw on the past, identify speaker roles and intent, knowledge-based inference generation, narration, retelling, coherence, and revision, to name a few (Majors, 2007).

In the public space of the salon, men, women, and adolescents actively constitute a kind of counter-public (Harris-Lacewell, 2004). Day-to-day obstacles and dilemmas encountered in the external world are shaken and sifted through a discerning mesh of social and ideological narratives. Collectively, members of this counter-public reread, reshape, rename, and redefine their experiences and place in the world—transforming the salon into an intellectual "arena" through a process of problem posing and problem solving. The result is an interpretive narrative critical of the world and the group (Harris-Lacewell, 2004). Talk, therefore, becomes a multivoiced, multiscripted text, and it is this text that guides, informs, and propels those who simultaneously create and witness it into action.

I've witnessed these transformations. As a child, my place was in the peripheral overflow of "seen-and-not-heard." There, I spent many Saturday mornings along with a handful of other tag-along children, witnessing our mothers come alive in gestures, tones, and attitudes. The ebb and flow of the performance can be so cohesive that a novice observer might well imagine that such beauty shop talk is carefully crafted and rehearsed, when in fact it is likely that the performers have never met before.

The robust nature of these verbal exchanges enthralled, transported, educated, and inspired me. So much so that in 1998, while completing my graduate studies, I began what would extend into a 6-year ethnographic and qualitative study of four African American hair salons in the Midwest and southern regions of the United States. In the process I realized that contributing to the persistence and vitality surrounding this local activity is a dynamic constellation of culturally situated, communicative means that participants draw on to cue a collective linguistic performance, convey and interpret meaning, understand and be understood (Bruner, 1990). Each participant's contribution defines and is defined by that of the others. Their exchange is constituted by specific African American speech conventions, rhetorical features, and worldviews, which simultaneously defy and affirm geographic, social class, and racialized borders (Abrahams, 1976; Bourdieu, 1977; Hill-Collins, 2000).

I began this book with the voice of Ms. Addie and other members of this public space in order to highlight the assumptions I make with regard to these verbal exchanges—which I argue are literate practices—and the skills required for participation. According to Langer (1987), literacy is an act, a way of thinking, not a set of skills. And it is a purposeful activity—people read, write, talk, and think about real ideas and information in order to ponder and extend what they know, to communicate with others, to present their points of view, and to understand and be understood. The kinds of literate skills that Ms. Addie and generations of other African Americans display are not neutral cognitive skills, but a sociocultural toolkit that includes systems of values, language, discourse structures, and modes of reasoning or making (mediating) meaning and constructing individual and shared identities in the public, social world (Lave, 1996; Rogoff, 2003).

For some readers, I imagine that the scenario above was entertaining, yet bears no correspondence to what it means to be literate or make use of literate skill. For others, the nature of the talk in the salon—its content, structure, and cultural nuances and niches—may be reminiscent of something familiar. Regardless of whether the above exchange speaks to an experience known to the reader, my belief is that it is part of a valuable cultural toolkit belonging to many who struggle with competing academic discourses. Unfortunately, however, few language and literacy researchers have advocated appropriately complex theoretical and methodological frames that situate literacy achievement beyond cultural deficits or within broader, complex sociohistorical, cultural, and community contexts (Lee, 2007; Nasir, 2011). Fewer have dealt with the question of where and how social practices that frame academic literacy events in the contexts of one's lived social world occur and for what purpose (Morrell & Duncan-Andrade, 2003). Even fewer have grappled with how to identify and document what constitutes these events (the meaning-making processes, structures, content, values, codes, and rules) as they function across the life span and move within and across various contexts (Gutierrez & Rogoff, 2003; Scribner, 1984). Individual educators instinctively may weave pieces of this knowledge into their practice, but much more than underground understanding is needed if we are going to teach all of our students in culturally appropriate and accessible ways.

As a site of cultural-community practice, the African American hair salon functions as a ritual setting, talk being a part of that ritual, where skilled, literate reasoning can and does occur through social dialogue. Undergirding this process are the attitudes, outlooks, and behaviors of the individuals. It is through the everyday practices and structure of the salon that a nexus of interrelated cultural models and belief systems is constructed. These complex performances of sense making play out in the cultural practices and themes that are tantamount to African American daily life (Harris-Lacewell, 2004). It is such performances, where individuals collectively share, create, and extend meanings, that drive my work, as they beg the more challenging question: Can a thorough ethnography and documentation of talk in the African American hair salon and barbershop relate to what goes on in formal instructional settings in schools and inform practice? The answer is yes!

Shoptalk: Lessons in Teaching from an African American Hair Salon has two aims: (1) to illustrate, through empirical data, a kind of talk that occurs in the culturally shared spaces that African Americans occupy, and (2) to detail how, within such talk, teaching, learning, and identity work occur and the strategies that are involved in doing so. The skills required of participants in order to read and interpret perspectives, while making sense of the worlds they traverse, are similar to what is required of students when they engage in interpretive tasks in the academic domain of literary response (Lee, 2007). I will present an analysis of talk that takes place in hair salons across multiple social spaces, indicating that adolescents/young adults who participate in the talk are socialized into (1) a participatory role within that discourse that includes collaboration, cultural norms, and values; (2) a process of reasoning through goal-oriented tasks that involve collaboration and an examination of multiple and often divergent perspectives; and (3) an interactive form of reasoned argumentation and problem solving that is both socially and cognitively beneficial.

This book offers an analysis of a culturally and socially situated language practice that occurs in the public space of the Black hair salon, but also moves beyond that space and into the urban classroom, to consider how we might apply the lessons learned. We will look specifically at the ways of speaking, performing, and reasoning within these contexts, where participants of discourse are supported in using their community-based language as a resource for disciplinary reasoning and problem solving. The analysis presented here illustrates how cultural-community-based discourse norms, and the structures and content of argumentation similar to those located in the hair salon, provide participation structures that invite engagement with complex problem solving (Au, 1980). This book also illustrates how language and culture interact to inform learning and teaching in ways that are unexpected by those who attempt to facilitate that process.

STRUCTURE OF THE BOOK

This book begins with Chapter 1: Needing to Know, Wanting to Teach, where I describe the experiences that led me to investigate the socially organized practices that characterize the African American hair salon as a space of teaching and learning. I describe the theoretical underpinnings that contribute to my understanding of how people talk to one another as an aspect of literate practice and the rationale behind the studies presented in this book.

In Chapter 2, Orienting Ourselves to Cultural Ways of Knowing, we will grapple with the question: *How might cultural ways of knowing enable us to confront assumptions regarding the limitations of everyday discourses in pursuit of academic knowledge?* It is in Chapter 2 that I present the hub of my research: a multilevel framework of Shoptalk. This framework brings together theory and methods from linguistics, anthropology, sociology, and sociocultural activity theory perspectives on schooling and cognitive perspectives on literacy learning.

In Chapter 3, Institutional Organization of Community Practice, I answer the question: *How are teaching and learning viewed in the context of the salon and what can that teach us?* This chapter will examine teaching and learning from the point of view of salon owner Darlene, who reports on her social positioning inside the salon as that of "teacher." This chapter draws the reader's attention to the formalization of the localized identities of the men and women who work in these salons.

In addition to homing in on the self-ascribed and imposed identities of members of this community, Chapter 3 examines the cultural and community forces that inform the processes and skill of work in each salon. In this chapter we take a closer look at the intersecting and sometimes conflicting views members hold with regard to what it means to teach and to learn within that context.

Chapter 4, Cultural Border Crossing and the Narration of Social Texts, grapples with the question: *What are the intersections between participation in discourse communities, problem solving, and social and academic identities?* I explore the instructional potential of a community hair salon as part and parcel of the processes of learning and identity formation. Chapter 4 details the ways in which both Darlene and Ms. Addie, a client and schoolteacher, linguistically navigate their social positions both within and outside the salon.

I report on interactions between both of the women and other members of the salon and how each strategically moves between her professional and cultural identities and values by both adopting and adapting institutional languages. For both Darlene and Ms. Addie, self-identification through language becomes more than the creation of categories for self and others; it becomes a tool for attending, to their advantage, to the understandings of other participants within the salon.

Chapter 5, What Gets Read, Who Is the Reader, and How Do You Talk Back to Disempowering Texts?, takes lessons from the community of teaching and learning in the salon to answer the question: *How, through Shoptalk, are youth able to consider alternative perspectives, take on roles within the argumentation, and digest (and even assume) multiple points of view—skills required in any language arts classroom?* I report on an event in which an adolescent makes a claim (before an audience of adult men and women) regarding her daughter's seeming failure to perform well at school. Undergirding this claim is the mother's account of an institutional (school) reading of her daughter's academic performance. A public response to the mother's claim is prompted when an adult participant shows an interest in the young mother and, along with other community members, attempts to engage her in a conversation. While the attempt to engage serves as a prompt for the young mother and brings the discussion of schooling to the floor, I argue that the nature of problem posing and problem solving provides an alternative mode of reasoning and argumentation structure to participants within the discourse.

Chapter 6, Shifting Borders and Landscapes, answers the question: *What shifts in paradigms must we make in order to cross borders of classroom and community?* In this chapter we look ahead to the classroom by calling upon teachers who struggle between competing notions of what counts as knowledge, in their own lived experiences and within curricular design and reform efforts, to consider such culturally shared and situated contexts, like the hair salon, as robust sites to elaborate and contest long-standing, popular notions of what it means to know and teach. At its core, this book is concerned with addressing the challenge of appropriating systems of activity across social and academic contexts. In Chapter 6, I shift the focus away from the context of the salon by looking toward the classroom, calling for the design of instructional learning environments and curriculum that make use of the prior knowledge that students bring into the classroom.

We will consider the instructional means and supports necessary to move beyond traditional models of classroom instruction and to include in that context the fuller experience of what it means to build knowledge as a member of the African American speech community. In Chapter 6 we will consider how traversing cultural academic borders involves an acknowledgment and explicit understanding of how one is both positioned by and a participant of multiple (institutional) discourse communities.

In Chapter 7, Shoptalk in the Classroom, I answer the question: *What does culturally responsive teaching and learning within problem-solving activities framed through Shoptalk look like within one urban language arts classroom?* This chapter articulates Shoptalk as a model for classroom instruction and formulates some guidelines for its use. I provide a description of a particular unit of instruction taught within an urban secondary language arts classroom. This instructional unit centers on my perspective of literacy as culturally situated, goal-oriented practice. This unit uses multiple strategies to help students deeply interrogate a short but challenging piece of culturally inflammatory text. Through this unit, which includes text analysis, conversation, journaling, role-playing, and debate, students are scaffolded to acquire and apply deeper language and thinking skills. I look specifically at ways of speaking, performing, and reasoning within this context, where students are supported in using their community-based language as a resource for disciplinary reasoning.

In Chapter 8, The Classroom as a Site of Guided Participation, I answer the question: *How do community-based discourse norms, structures, and content of argumentation (similar to those located in the hair salon) provide participation structures that invite engagement with complex problem solving?* Chapter 8 illustrates how students take hold of the floor in order to counter or debate an institutional point of view. Students' ability to establish and maintain their positionings within the participation framework, however, is contingent upon previous apprenticeships in that kind of cultural talk. I will show how Shoptalk, as a way of seeing and a way of doing, enabled students to establish their culturally situated positionings and certify their own knowledge.

This book concludes in Chapter 9, Conclusion: Knowing Where You've Been to Know Where You Are Going, with a consideration of the educational implications for this body of research. In addition to tying together the analyses presented in previous chapters, my discussion summarizes the study, relating those findings in the hair salons and classroom to previous findings in the field of language, literacy, and culture.

CHAPTER 1

Needing to Know, Wanting to Teach

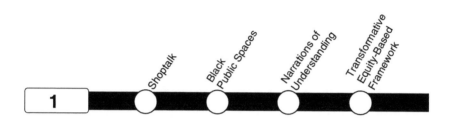

Making a case for the role that everyday discourses can play in service to classroom teaching and learning.

Kuttin' Up hair salon is where I met Ms. Addie and the many other folks whose storied voices lend themselves to this book. Hidden in a tiny corner on the 12th floor of the Pittsfield Office Building in downtown Chicago just one block west of "the Magnificent Mile," the unassuming Black hair salon, once noticed, stands out against the backdrop of the historically White, upper class affluence that characterizes the district.

During my 2 years documenting talk at Kuttin' Up, I observed that many of the "regulars" were either members of the same Pentecostal church, or closely acquainted with it in some way. Although the church itself was located miles away in the Near North Side community known best for what was once the Cabrini Green Housing Project, its presence and influence was near, and lent to a kind of sermonic overflow that defied borders and effortlessly flowed into the salon. You could observe this in the artifacts outlining the space—beginning with gospel music emanating from the radio, to the Christian tracts that intermingled with *Ebony*, *Jet*, and *Black Hair Today* magazines lining the table in the waiting area. Every 15 minutes or so a symphony of hair dryers, running water, and testimonials would be disrupted by the earthshaking rumblings of the "Green Line" L train running along the building's western edge, transporting its occupants across geographic and social borders.

I've ridden this L train hundreds of times, maybe more. Over the years, and during the course of my study of talk in the salon and classroom, I have found inspiration in this and similar Chicago Transit Authority (CTA) train lines. Its maps posted on the platform display an intricate, color-coded, and deliberate set of lines that directionally traverse this sprawling city's borders of race, class, and social relations. As such, riders from all walks of life interface with diverse geography, people, and social phenomena, which are largely reflective of the section of the city in which the train is traveling. Figure 1.1 draws on this map as a metaphor, my concept of Shoptalk as it traverses space and time, moving through communities, each a picturesque representation of the social world order (and dis-order), harmony, and dis-harmony (Kazembe, 2012).

This stratified social order is constructed through a series of tacit agreements and mediated by images, tales, and scripts. Riding these trains you can observe the disparate, physical condition of the train stations and commerce—kiosks, coffee stations, and newspaper stands. Thus, the commute is a subtle social commentary on the political and social economy of the city, moving through a complex, interwoven maze of social inequality, privileging, and cultural interaction. Riders, for their part, have the opportunity to read and interrogate the commuting experience, through a kind of *cultural border crossing*, where people actively move across the socially, culturally, and politically constructed divides that separate cultural groups and discourse communities (Anzaldua, 1987; Majors, 2014; Majors & Orellana, 2003).

In the chapters that follow you and I will cross several borders: (1) the social and cultural borders that exist within and across institutions, (2) the linguistic and ideological borders that penetrate and inform in-school and out-of-school discourse practices, and (3) the pedagogical borders of narrative practices that influence teaching, learning, and transformative action. We will examine, perhaps trouble, what it means to know and what it means to teach in the competing contexts of cultural-community and institutional "safety" that undermine notions of care and reinforce status quo equity within the classroom (Gay, 2000; Leonardo & Porter, 2010). In doing so, we invariably will raise more questions. For while the act of border crossing is fundamentally a personal choice, the nature of that choice characterizes our nation's unmet promise—that education will be made available to all on equal terms, so that every member of this society can realize a productive life and contribute to the greater welfare (Darling-Hammond, 2010)—as either imperative or ironic. Hence, for many classroom teachers, knowing and teaching is the tacit maintenance of numerous propositions, theories, assumptions, and false perceptions regarding the lives of their students as they, like the train beyond the salon window, move through spaces of what it means to know and what it means to teach.

Figure 1.1. Shoptalk Metro Lines

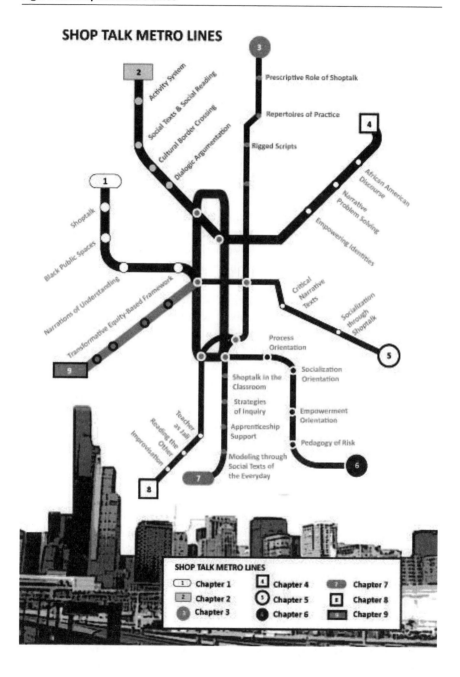

SHOP TALK METRO LINES

Prescriptive Role of Shoptalk
Repertoires of Practice
Rigged Scripts
Activity System
Social Texts & Social Reading
Cultural Border Crossing
Dialogic Argumentation
Shoptalk
Black Public Spaces
Narrations of Understanding
Transformative Equity-Based Framework
African American Discourse
Narrative Problem Solving
Empowering Identities
Critical Narrative Texts
Socialization through Shoptalk
Process Orientation
Shoptalk in the Classroom
Strategies of Inquiry
Apprenticeship Support
Modeling through Social Texts of the Everyday
Socialization Orientation
Empowerment Orientation
Pedagogy of Risk
Teacher as Self
Reading the Other
Improvisation

SHOP TALK METRO LINES
1 Chapter 1 4 Chapter 4 7 Chapter 7
2 Chapter 2 5 Chapter 5 8 Chapter 8
3 Chapter 3 6 Chapter 6 9 Chapter 9

SHIFTING THE DEFICIT DISCOURSE

The voices we will encounter in the following ·chapters are those of African American men, women, and adolescents engaged in talk "Shoptalk"—a specific genre of conversational discourse through which teaching and learning are mediated. Anchored in the premise that both teaching and learning take place within a complex sociocultural ecology and are filtered through cultural screens that teachers, students, and researchers bring to the classroom, the research presented here is an attempt to disrupt and reimagine what it means to become caring, culturally responsive instructors for ethnically diverse students (Gay, 2000). My decision to frame Shoptalk as an act of cultural border crossing stems from (1) the discourse and assumptions surrounding the critical problems relating to student achievement; (2) the appropriation of cultural "funds of knowledge" (Moll & Greenberg, 1990, p. 322) in the classroom; and (3) the question of how teachers can leverage cultural-community practices and instructional approaches (Hollins, 1996). These issues meet at an intersection in urban U.S. classrooms populated predominantly by students of color and teaching populations that hold diverse perceptions, political beliefs, and attitudes toward culture and learning. The focus of this study and intervention in which I was involved (Lee, 1992, 1993, 2005, 2007; Lee & Majors, 2003) and on which earlier work is based (Majors, 2001, 2003, 2004, 2006; Majors & Ansari, 2009) is the domain of responses to literature. This present work builds on the findings of Lee's Cultural Modeling project intervention in order to further the case for the enabling potential of particular kinds of non-normative discourses within the classroom (Lee, 2005, 2007).

Shoptalk in the classroom was a part of an intervention in a low-performing public charter school that took place over the course of 4 years, from 2004 to 2008. As part of the project, I taught a high school English language arts class each year of the intervention. A curriculum was designed for the teaching of literature according to the principles of Cultural Modeling and observations of Shoptalk in the urban hair salon. The high school juniors and seniors in the classes were African American adolescents, speakers of African American Vernacular English, and academically underachieving in terms of standardized reading scores.

This analysis of talk in both the salon and classroom is significant. It aims to propel classroom teaching and learning forward through the consideration of the culturally and socially embedded norms for attacking problems that students bring into the classroom, and consequently the consideration of the pedagogical supports that speak to those norms. At this intersection are two challenges. The first involves making explicit the social and cognitive dimensions of the problem-solving task at hand. The second involves the acknowledgment of the multiple and dynamic ways that teachers and students respond to pedagogical supports that are cultural in nature. Overcoming these challenges involves locating successful ways of fusing literacy teaching and learning with culturally aware and relevant instruction (Lee & Majors, 2003). Whereas these aims are important, this present work attempts to deal with the often overly simplified and highly generalized notion of culture and its complex characteristics that afford opportunities for making sense not just of written and oral texts, but of the world and how culture—as an aspect of the world—has continuance in practices outside the immediate home and community.

This book makes the case for cultural practices that inform how we think about culturally responsive teaching and learning and what can be done in order to accomplish that. It concerns itself with talk—talk that is multivoiced, multiscripted, and action provoking. Harnessing such talk across community and classroom supports teaching and learning, advancing students' interpretive skills, collaborative sense making, problem solving, and personal and collective empowerment. Personal experience, theoretical assertions, research findings, and best practices suggest that at "the heart of the educational process is the interactions that occur between teachers and students" (Gay, 2000, p. 47). Hence, this book deals with talk and action. In doing so, it speaks back to persistent and violent deficit-based pedagogies, which pervade an increasingly complicated landscape of schooling in the urban community. Such pedagogies, and the ideologies that inform them, seep into administrative meetings, hallway exchanges, and, most importantly, the intellectual performance of students most at risk.

In presenting this research I hope that I might shift, or at least nudge, the discourse surrounding achievement in a different direction. Arguably, such a shift can influence a broadening in our understanding of the learning potential and processes of all students, a push-back against persistent and oppressive classroom practices imposed upon people who are most at risk, and an alternative to the limitations of achievement gap discourse. In doing so, perhaps I might shed new light on what it means to know and to teach from a perspective of cultural resources and not cultural lack.

CULTURALLY SHARED AND SITUATED BLACK PUBLIC SPACE

Like barbershops for men, the local hair salon is a culturally shared and situated *Black public space* where during the course of the everyday, people come together "to organize around communal problems; sit together to cut and style one another's hair; pass news about one another through oral and written networks; and use music, style, and humor to communicate with one another (Harris-Lacewell, 2004, p. 1). It is also a space where contested identities, alternative points of view, and culturally informed structures for participation and argumentation are situated within the context of the African American community (Hill-Collins, 2000). Such oral and communal patterns of dialogue and engagement contribute to the distinctiveness of the Black hair salon as a ritual counter-public space, discourse being a part of that ritual.

This distinction, however, is shared with other "separate, indigenous, race-based institutions at the local community level" (Harris-Lacewell, 2004, p. 7), like the Black church, fraternal organizations, online outlets, and markets, which together constitute a collective "sphere of critical practices and visionary politics . . . which individuals can join with the energies of the street, the school, the church, and the city to constitute a challenge to the worldviews and exclusionary violence of much public space in the United States" (Black Public Sphere Collective, 1995, quoted in Harris-Lacewell, 2004, p. 5). As one aspect of the African American counter-public sphere, the Black hair salon is a constant, clearly defined physical space in the community, within which lies an autonomous, socially and culturally safe space for its members, whose perceptions are made public and governed by the discourse norms of the culture (Jacobs-Huey, 1997a).

This study of talk in the salon and classroom focuses on the act of social reading and on the notion of a common African American experience through the public performances of African American women and youth jointly involved in Shoptalk. Shoptalk, as a kind of conversational discourse, socializes individuals into routine problem-solving strategies to navigate the complex world (Majors, 2003, 2004, 2007). In short, a young adult participating in Shoptalk might pose a social dilemma with which he or she is dealing, emphasizing its potential consequences. Women and men within the hair salon, through narrative, would "re-direct" (Scribner, 1984) the initial dilemma in nonthreatening ways that afforded multiple perspectives from which to view it. As a consequence, youth come to consider alternative perspectives, take on roles within the argumentation, and take up multiple points of view.

Unlike traditional narratives that position the teller as distanced, removed from the context and unaffected, narratives told within Shoptalk are reflexive, liberatory, and dialogic, embracing both the local (near to) and distal (far from). Findings framed within these narratives lend themselves to a kind of discourse that is noted in spaces of teaching and learning that are culturally shared and situated. This kind of discourse affirms certain behaviors, attitudes, and performances of all those in the event as being culturally shared, productive, meaningful, and valued. Rather than fostering a blind spot (aka color-blindness), this discourse creates a liberatory space for a kind of knowing that is powerful (Leonardo & Porter, 2010). In effect, the routine nature of the talk within the salon, as well as the social histories the women share, act as social supports that potentially, over time, influence prototypical coping responses, particularly for the young women in the salon (Majors, 2007). Shoptalk grounds itself in the theory of everyday talk, and posits that

> Although none of the individuals engaging in the conversation will be instantly convinced by the arguments of others, all will be affected by their participation in this conversation. Each person who has shared in this interaction will adjust his or her . . . [attitudes] to the extent that he or she is convinced by the various arguments made. (Harris-Lacewell, 2004, p. 12)

While very often adolescents and young adults were the impetus for such socializing routines, data show that older adult women were more likely to be involved in these forms of argumentation, which afford alternative perspectives. Additionally, such routines are grounded in a recurring discourse, which frames opportunities for all participants to develop problem-solving scripts and approaches for attacking similar problems. It is the robustness of the routine problem-solving outcomes that warrants adapting similar discourses to a new setting, namely, the classroom.

DISCOURSE TRAVERSING COMMUNITY AND CLASSROOM

If our aim is to improve educational outcomes for racial and ethnic minority youth and for youth facing persistent generational poverty, we cannot continue to ignore students' and community members' perceptions of what is threatening to and what is supportive of their own development (Lee, Spencer, & Harpalani, 2003). Hence, drawing from this body of ethnographic research, I began to develop a literacy tool for my own classroom using videotaped vignettes and transcriptions of hair salon interactions to guide my design.

By examining novice enculturation into the salon, we are able to unpack the role of thought and language in the acquisition and appropriation of skill in problem solving. Critical discourse analysis (CDA) provides a useful lens for considering the complex relations between the social construction of text, both oral and written, and the maintenance/disruption of power. As a theoretical and methodological tool, CDA draws our attention to both the social processes and structures within the discourse that give rise to narrative improvisation. Inherent in this view are the interconnected concepts of power, history, and ideology. In addition, CDA draws our attention to how the capacities to deploy different linguistic and paralinguistic codes and registers, including African American English (AAE), act as mediational thinking tools through which participants in activity communicate to achieve particular goals (Gee, 1992, 1993; Gee, Hull, & Lankshear, 1996). Within the African American English tradition, for example, are linguistic folk traditions that contribute to the discourse, such as folklore, folk utterances, songs, and tales of folk expression, and that comprise verbal strategies, rhetorical devices, and folk expressive rituals that derive from a mutually understood notion of modes of discourse.

Discourses from this perspective are viewed as "ways of behaving, interacting, valuing, thinking, believing, speaking, writing and 'reading' that are accepted instantiations of particular roles by specific groups of people" (Hull & Schultz, 2002, p. 21). A view of discourse as social practice enables me to consider the "text in context" (van Dijk, 1977) as well as the very complex roles, social identities, and social perspectives from which people are invited (summoned) to speak, listen, act, read, write, read, think, feel, and value in certain characteristic, historically recognizable ways in combination with their own individual styles and creativity (Bourdieu, 1977, 1991; Foucault, 1980; Gee et al., 1996). "Describing discourse as social practice implies a dialectical relationship between a particular discursive event and situations, institutions(s) and social structures which frame it: the discursive event is shaped by . . . [the women in the salon], but it also shapes them" (Wodak, 1996, p. 15).

Critical literacy studies (CLS) offers a second set of conceptual lenses for understanding social texts and the reading of social relations. CLS addresses literacies as situated within sociocultural practices, discourse as connected to culturally situated notions of power, and texts as functioning to represent certain ideologies (Barton & Hamilton, 1998; Gee, 1997; Lankshear, 1997; Street, 2000). CLS highlights the fact that literacy practices are not neutral cognitive skills, but social and cultural tools for making meaning, constructing identities, and representing ideologies in the social world.

People enact ideologies, which are coherent constellations of values, beliefs, and practices that impose an order on the world. Ideologies are used to compete for dominance and some become more prevalent and more dominant than others. Those that are dominant serve the dominating classes, or those in power (Fairclough, 1995). Not only are ideologies established as an ordering of the world, but dominant ideologies become all-encompassing and "natural" so that we take them for granted. Thus, they become hegemonic, structuring conceptions of the world even for those who are marginalized and oppressed in the face of dominant ideological views (Gramski, 1971). One of the first steps in practicing critical consciousness, a goal of critical literacy (Freire, 1993), is to problematize the way things are and to recognize it as actually one of many possibilities of the way things could be.

This perspective informs my understanding of literacy practices as well as the focus on cultural narratives in this book. As Gilbert (1992) argues, narratives "have a functional role in our culture: we live a good deal of our lives on the power of various stories, and it is through stories that we position ourselves in relation to others, and are ourselves positioned by the stories of our culture" (p. 213). According to Bruner (1990), our sense of the normative is nourished in narrative, but so is our "sense of breach and exception" (p. 12). The oral narratives that I examine in this book provide a space through which identities can be constructed and expressed as well as resisted and reshaped.

TRANSFORMATIVE-EQUITY-BASED FRAMEWORK FOR INSTRUCTION

My work in the classroom is a response to a call put forth by scholars in the field of critical race theory (Crenshaw et al., 1995; Delgado & Stefancic, 2000; Guinier & Torres, 2002; Ladson-Billings, 1998, 2005). In this post–*Brown v. Board* era, failure to account for the historical nature of the classroom context constitutes an "interest convergence" (Bell, 2004), whereas the urban classroom objective would appear to advance the interests of White elites, with minority students and faculty left with little incentive (or support) to eradicate (challenge) it. Similarly, within the ideological framework of schooling, institutional racism still lies unexamined, buried in the underlying assumptions that shape many classroom curricula.

This status quo curriculum doesn't address classroom tensions, hierarchies, and ideologies that impact pedagogy and the ability to deliver curriculum. Canadian feminist scholar Srivastava (2005) uses the term *nonracist* to refer to "a liberal discourse of equality" (p. 35). Such a discourse positions the classroom as not connecting existent racist structures to the everyday language and sociomaterial acts that support and reify them. Equity is a step, but it is not enough. Exploring the complicated and nuanced issues of culture, class, and racial identity within the classroom is an essential component of culturally responsive and culturally relevant instruction. This imperative becomes increasingly clear as the racial divide continues to grow between White teacher and Black student in the urban classroom. It is not enough to make claims to equity-based frameworks if underlying color-blind, nonracist discourses and practices remain at the foundation of curriculum and (Srivastava, 2005). First and foremost, a color-blind discourse serves to calcify White supremacist ideals, privileging their normalized cultural and intellectual practices. For this reason an attempt to achieve educational equity through classroom practices must move beyond the discourse of nonracism and enact antiracist action, a political philosophy and practice committed to challenging racism as systemic in institutions and everyday life.

A transformative-equity-based framework goes a step beyond the status quo nonracist discourse, to draw on antiracist action. Shoptalk, when practiced in the classroom as a site of critical resistance, can provide robust learning practices that are simultaneously humanizing, race-conscious, and equity-oriented. According to Banks (1998), the aims of the transformative approach to education are to teach students to think critically and to develop the skills to formulate, document, and justify their conclusions by challenging dominant assumptions and illuminating collisions of ideas—the nondominant and the dominant—throughout the curriculum. Such an approach affords students opportunities to engage in critical thinking and to develop more reflective perspectives about what they are learning. The approach pushes students to look with the head and the heart as they critically examine issues both inside and outside the classroom (Morrell & Duncan-Andrade, 2003).

Many factors enter into how I engage the practice of Shoptalk in the classroom. Drawing on Banks's (1998, 2001) proposition for a transformative framework, my own pedagogical approach is intended to encourage future teachers to understand and confront their own cultural and social spaces, ideological development, and, more important, their privileged positions as contexts of learning and identity development. Such a pedagogy must take into account not only how our cultures shape our practices but how we respond to what we perceive as our cultural uniqueness and the accompanying racialized and gendered agendas (Lee & Johnson-Bailey, 2004). Part and parcel of this transformative-equity-based framework is the focus on critical self-reflection in which students examine issues from various perspectives that impact their lives. In an attempt to address the discourse of teaching toward multicultural awareness, this approach encourages teachers to confront their own cultural spaces as sites of ideological development.

The implementation of a transformative-equity-based curriculum design extends the challenge of how educators respond to the call for culturally responsive practices. While equity-based education encourages students to be conversant with an increasingly global and hierarchical societal structure, it is also a significant move forward in taking a step toward the initial promise of *Brown v. Board of Education* (1954). Such a first step, hopefully, will create a population of students who in their own communities can model the equity-based framework as a liberatory practice. Furthermore, the urban classroom calls attention to how race and racism enter into our subjectivities and ideological stances. Hence, the classroom and the ensuing curriculum serve as a catalyst for the manifestation of underlying and sometimes repressed assumptions.

A transformative-equity-based framework is invested in rethinking what it means to teach and reinvigorates the notion of liberation and transformation. Cultural socialization is invested in utilizing difference as a robust space for learning (Coard, Wallace, Stevenson, & Brotman, 2004; Stevenson & Davis, 2004). The neutralization of race, and consequently the erasure, so to speak, of cultural epistemologies, is what a transformative-equity-based framework and cultural socialization seek to resist. Keeping that in mind, the processes of socialization include an analysis of structures of power, participation, and language in discourse, as well as social interactions observed. These social interactions include the role of participants, enactments of point of view, the authority of participants as mutually constructed and shared, and, finally, what counts as knowledge.

As a transformative-equity-based framework, Shoptalk resists public discourses of sameness and conformity, and addresses issues of identity that impact teaching and learning with regard to cultural-minority-group members in particular, and African Americans specifically. The collection of voices that follow is meant to invite an awareness of a kind of engagement that constitutes a hybrid space where participants appear to reject prescribed formats for determining what gets read and who can be the reader, in favor of improvisational and scripted ways of talking back, redefining, and confronting problems. Through narrative traditions, social actors like Ms. Addie reason about and represent the canonical—those values, ideals, and ways of acting and thinking that are institutionalized in cultural histories. In this sense, narrative functions as a vehicle by which to reflect, represent, and create systems of understanding and valuing for individuals in specific contexts, in which they understand themselves in relation to the world. Participants and nonparticipants (which often include youth) "develop a means for expressing and understanding who they are through their routine participation in culturally organized narrative practices in which personal experiences are recounted . . . [and those] narratives of personal experience may be particularly useful as a means of gaining access to implicit propositions about the self" (Miller, Potts, Fung, Hoogstra, & Mintz, 1990, p. 308).

Enactment of Shoptalk in the classroom draws from a transformative-equity-based framework in that it:

- Requires critical self-reflection on part of the instructor and the students
- Enables students to examine issues from multiple perspectives
- Encourages teachers to confront their own cultural spaces as sites of ideological development and privileged positions

The design of the Shoptalk curriculum is the space where the particular discourses of equity-based education, socialization, and literacy intersect. The mechanisms for youth socialization reside within and are developed according to a set of goals that are defined by the transformative-equity-based framework. These curricular goals are integrated by our understanding of literacy and learning. Research related to language and learning has shown that success and failure in school is contingent upon one's ability to regulate and situate identities, utilize culturally developed tools, and negotiate models of meaning in shared social activity. However, many language-minority students lack such success, struggling with conflicts between, on the one hand, their primary and community-based identities and existing personal models of the world instantiated through community-based discourses, and, on the other, discrepant new constructs and literate discourses (Gee, 2000).

Some interrogations have led to meaningful classroom practices and a broadening in the landscape of education. This is insufficient, however, as many have tended to be too narrow and specialized, limiting useful responses to schooling and the fields that generated them (Langer, 1987). Furthermore, such investigations often have gone uncontested, been situated solely within the context of the classroom, and generated a recurrence of popular themes and characterizations of literate practices. This not only has led to an underconceptualization of issues, but more important, it has led to a lack of consideration and understanding with regard to learning, its relationship to who people are—their cultural ways of doing—and the societies and institutions they encounter and create.

Many under-represented students continue to experience dissonance—marginalization and academic failures within school systems. In fact, culturally responsive teaching and learning are in no way akin to the multicultural celebration of food, folks, and fun at school. Rather, this work calls for the design of instructional spaces that align participation structures and strategies from students' everyday experiences with generative disciplinary knowledge and literate skill. Contingent upon the development of useful problem-solving strategies (domain-specific and social) are the connections made between students' everyday readings of the world and the text that they encounter in the classroom. The domain-specific strategies for encountering text are also part of the tradition of narrative meaning-making that is part of many students' cultural toolkit, as will be illustrated in later chapters of this book.

Missing from the educational landscape are replicable participation structures and processes of reasoning that members of the communities engage in and how these illustrations are put to use in the classroom. In addition to an examination of talk in the African American hair salon, we examine my work in an English language arts classroom where I've documented African American students' uses of community-based funds of knowledge and African American discourse norms as tools for the construction of complex literary arguments, much like those that occur in the salon. Such arguments often are represented through narrative and call on such skills as revision, improvisation, and inferencing, to name a few.

This book illustrates students' own considerations of the themes embedded within the arguments that you would find taking place in the salon, through structures similar to those that frame the discourse of Shoptalk as a part of a disciplinary language arts unit. In so doing, this research confronts assumptions regarding the limitations of everyday discourses in pursuit of academic knowledge. It further explores relationships between participation in discourse communities and academic identities for students historically underserved by public education in the United States.

CHAPTER 2

Orienting Ourselves to Cultural Ways of Knowing

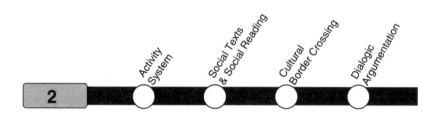

How might cultural ways of knowing enable us to confront assumptions regarding the limitations of everyday discourses in pursuit of academic knowledge?

Picture this: A young woman, hair newly washed and set in curlers, sits cross-legged, patiently thumbing the latest issue of *Essence* magazine. Between flips, she reaches up to adjust the plastic cap that insulates her conditioner-soaked hair against the blast of hot air emitting from the hood of the dryer. Seated and standing nearby are men, women, and youth of varying ages. A toddler crouches at the foot of a chair, amusing herself with a colorful array of curling rods, hairpins, and combs. The owner and lead stylist of the salon, Wendi, who provided these tools for the child's short-lived amusement, deftly and precisely snips the straightened ends of her client's shoulder-length hair.

Among those present is Ms. Addie, an elementary school teacher and avid reader. Beneath the whir of hair dryers, the buzzing of clippers, and echoes of conversations spattered across the room, Jackie (Wendi's assistant) and Carmen (a longtime regular client of Wendi's) are curiously eyeing Ms. Addie's attire: heavy black military boots, a sweeping floor-length, red and white chambray checkered skirt, long layered lace slip, white-breasted apron, long-sleeved white cotton shirt buttoned to the top with a rounded Peter Pan collar, and to finish it off a white kerchief tied at the top to cover her hair. The conversation that began earlier (see Introduction) continues:

Ms. Addie: You know, I went to a workshop at the Newberry library on Saturday morning and they had all of these teachers. I mean, this is a Saturday morning and people came and they turned some people away because the room was too small. But the one thing that they were trying to stress was that we were coming together to develop concepts about how to teach about slavery.

From the audience: Mmmm.

Ms. Addie: And these folks, there was this one woman there who was White. And another one, a young Black woman. And they happened to be sitting on the same couch. One on one end, one on the other end. And so this guy said, "Is there anyone here who is having difficulty with this subject?" And so this one woman raised her hand and she said, "You know, I'm having difficulty because I teach the 6th grade, but I feel guilty, I, um, my family owned slaves.

From the audience: Girrrlll. . . . Mmmm. (exaggerated eye rolling and eyebrow raising)

Ms. Addie: And she said, "I have all of the books, I know how many people were sold, even their names. How much it cost. How much they paid for them."

Carmen: She's got everybody in a book, huh?

Ms. Addie: And everybody was looking at her. It's in her family.

From the audience: Hmm.

Carmen: In her family? I hear you.

Ms. Addie: And she's like—she looks, she looks like she may be in her late 40s, if that old, and she said, "And I feel so guilty and I don't know what to do about it." And so then this other lady, the young lady, said—the other Black lady said, "Why?" She says, "I feel guilty because," she says, "I feel uncomfortable because I, I've only been teaching 4 years, and I don't, I don't want to teach the kids in a way where the kids will become angry. I want to teach it so that it's—it's objective, they will learn from it." And, uh, so these two—but after these two people said what they said—'cuz you could see the tension in the air. There was all kind of people, Black people, Hispanic people, and Jewish people—uh, but it was a kinda in the air, it was tension. But after these two people said what they said, it just cleared the air. It was an awesome class and I am so glad I went because this is a problem in America. Teachers who say they feel uncomfortable teaching about slavery.

SHOPTALK

The voices represented above are those of people engaging in *Shoptalk—a specific genre of conversational discourse through which teaching and learning are mediated in the context of the hair salon.* Shoptalk emerges out of Black public spaces and may include:

- Publicly performed, private conversations occurring in culturally shared situated sites of labor
- A sharing of personal experience often in narrative form
- Speakers evoking a certain image and assuming roles before an audience
- Talk functioning as a prescriptive tool, allowing the stylists to treat their clients' psychological and aesthetic needs
- Engaging forms of talk being communicated through AAE discourse norms (call and response, signifying, narrative argumentation)
- Oral narratives of personal experience and storytelling produced and interpreted through "acting" participants, generally for the purpose of providing resources, problem solving, and/or building knowledge
- Participants holding participation status as speakers and hearers within the participation framework

Shoptalk focuses not so much on the location of the talk but rather on the actions of participants within that cultural setting.

Before you and I continue to eavesdrop on Ms. Addie's conversation, imagine for a moment that we are first standing together on the elevated, or L, train platform (see Figure 2.1) somewhere near the intersection of what it means to know and to teach. At this intersection, Shoptalk serves as a resource, our boarding pass, if you will. Once on board you, other riders, and I can interrogate, contest, and make sense of the world.

I will continue to use the metaphor of public transit throughout this book as a way of navigating our journey.

Just like the L train, Shoptalk moves through space and time, shifting in form and function, acting as noun and verb. As a way of seeing (noun), Shoptalk invites us to consider *talk as performance in a system of activity,* where participants collaboratively make use of social and cultural tools in order to convey particular meanings in response to their social and academic readings (Majors & Ansari, 2009). As a way of doing (verb), Shoptalk is the process by which speakers engage with one another in problem-solving tasks and transform in/through their participation.

Figure 2.1. Riding the Chicago Transit System

I view Shoptalk as a *conceptual lens* that helps us consider and understand the complexity of teaching and learning. I view teaching and learning as an *activity*, in that my focus is on the system of interpersonal engagements and arrangements that are part of a process of individual and group knowledge building (Rogoff, 1995). Such interpersonal engagements and arrangements within the salon, for example, involve clients and stylists as social actors. Each social actor brings to his or her interactions shared cultural and social norms, such as values, goals, and language.

I also view Shoptalk as a *pedagogical (teaching) instrument*, in part to appropriate the forms of guided participation (redirecting through improvised argumentation) that occur in culturally shared spaces (Rogoff, 1995). Similarly, in the AAE-dominant classroom, teachers and students, as social actors, bring to their interactions cultural norms for participation. Some non-African American teachers learn and adopt some of these norms in the non-AAE-dominant classroom, but not all do so. Non-African American teachers, or those who do not participate in AAE discourses, can use the principles of Shoptalk to open the learning space to these norms of participation, without being members of the cultural community. In Shoptalk, shared cultural and social norms determine how participants engage with problems. Such norms shape people's interactions with other members of the activity. Hence, Shoptalk is a way of seeing and a way of doing.

As a way of seeing (*conceptual lens*), Shoptalk invites the observer to consider talk as performance in a system of activity, where participants collaborate and make use of cultural tools to convey particular meanings in response to their readings of word and world. The investigation of Shop-talk becomes the basis of understanding how individuals make sense of the world (our train ticket), rather than simply the surface details that we try to get past (Rogoff, 1995). From this perspective, the sociocultural activity of individuals, in relation to their cultural niches, is not lost in the landscape of research that far too often limits our attention to either the individual or the environment (Gutierrez & Rogoff, 2003; Lave & Wenger,1991; Rogoff, 2003). More important, however, Shoptalk serves as a lens for consider-ing what it means to know and to teach in culturally responsive ways, and offers rich insights into how urban African American youth, as members of their community, make use of particular funds of knowledge that in-clude critical reasoning skills that can be useful in communication, conflict resolution, resilience, and in-school/out-of-school literacy practices. When leveraged in the classroom, Shoptalk may provide an alternative space that structures opportunities for students to sort through the real-life dilemmas that they are expected to take up, *as well as* work through academic tasks, like identifying and solving problems in literature.

SETTING THE STAGE:
A SOCIOCULTURAL VIEW OF ACTIVITY IN THE SALON

The purposeful *actions* of participants of Shoptalk are grounded in a set of theoretical and methodological *assumptions*. Among these is a vibrant constellation of structures, norms, values, rules, and means for uses of talk, as well as the role that each speaker plays. As seen in Figure 2.2, these ele-ments constitute participants' engagement and direct their actions within the local setting.

Participants share and exchange cultural funds of knowledge through talk that traverses across contexts. Social actors—the participants and non-participants of Shoptalk—are identified as members of the overall structure of the activity. Ratified (accepted) participants of Shoptalk are entitled and expected to be a part of the communicative event. Unratified participants are not expected to take part and often adhere to a kind of restraint set by standards for events in which expression is seen as having little or no func-tional role.

Within each activity structure (salon or classroom), an interactional space is identified. This space consists of multiple activity systems, each con-stituted by the orientation of each particular task at hand, the norms for talk through which the task is communicated and carried out, artifacts, goals, and social/cognitive resources of the participants of the interaction and the roles assumed by them. The assumptions orienting each activity system are

Figure 2.2. Sociocultural Activity System

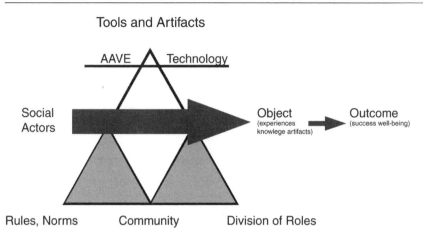

the rules and means for uses of talk, as well as the role that each participant plays within the activity of that space. These rules for talk and participants' roles are the cultural and social values that constitute the guidance referred to in Rogoff's (1995) concept of guided participation—the process and systems of involvement between people as they communicate and coordinate efforts while participating in culturally valued activity.

NAVIGATING SHOPTALK

Figure 2.3 illustrates how Shoptalk takes into account Rogoff's three "planes of analysis" (Rogoff, 1990).[1] Each plane of focus bears in mind a particular orientation and related goals, assumptions, habits of mind, and procedural rules toward a given task. In my consideration of sociocultural activity in both the salon and classroom, I account for three interconnected orientations of the problem-solving task—process, product, and socialization—and their intended goals, along each plane.

Process Orientation

In the first orientation, actions of participants are for the purpose of teaching a process or a particular task, and providing instruction through conversation in everyday situations where directives are embedded in the talk. For example, a client (as novice) may inquire as to the best way to style his or her hair, and the stylist (as expert) might respond with a series of steps the client can take to achieve that particular style. Here the stylist is like teacher

Figure 2.3. Planes of Analysis

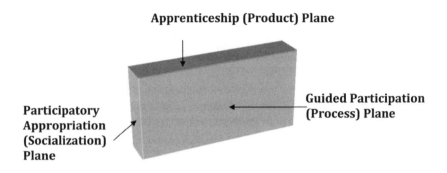

Apprenticeship (Product) Plane

Participatory Appropriation (Socialization) Plane

Guided Participation (Process) Plane

and she uses talk to convey certain procedures pertaining to hair care. Steps of a task are hierarchically and logically presented. The client, like a student, listens to and observes how the steps are executed, with the intent of repro-ducing them at some future time.

This *process orientation* serves two overarching functions, one of which resembles the initial consultation that Mike Rose speaks of in *The Mind at Work* (2004), in which dialogue acts as a kind of script (Schank & Abelson, 1977) between the stylist and client, and is critical to ensure that the client understands how the style in question will look on a particular head of hair. During the consultation it is absolutely imperative, suggests Rose (2004), that the stylist use "common, non-technical language" (p. 43), ask clarify-ing questions, and incorporate visuals to ensure that the client understands what the style is and how to achieve it. When viewed through the lens of Shoptalk, talk displayed during the consultation establishes procedural un-derstanding between stylist and client. It also serves a second function of creating a dynamic rapport and relationship between the individuals.

Product Orientation

Shifting from one plane to another, we keep this process orientation in the background as we zoom in on the next—a *product orientation*, where the target of instruction is increased staff performance rather than instruction. Research has shown that the formal institutional view for *apprenticing* new employees into practices in the salon is not always aligned with what or how something actually is learned, or even what may be considered useful by the learner for producing particular outcomes. When we direct our attention to the cultural tools people use to perform tasks and to meet their goals, the connections between individual, group and community processes become more transparent. This is important to note, particularly because contexts for learning (which include the workplace) are immanently hybrid: poly-contextual, multivoiced, and multiscripted (Gutierrez, Baquedano-Lopez, Tejeda, & Rivera, 1999). What is more, such hybridity may be the result of not only cooperation but also tensions, deviation from norms, conflicts, and resolutions that lend themselves to learning.

Socialization

In addition to the process and product orientations there is a *socialization orientation*, where the target is racial and cultural socialization among youth. *Racial socialization* is characterized as the developmental processes by which children acquire the behaviors, perceptions, values, and attitudes of an ethnic group, and come to see themselves and others as members of the group (Arnett, 1995; Bowman & Howard, 1985; Boykin & Ellison, 1995; Frabutt, Walker, & MacKinnon-Lewis, 2002; Hilliard, 1995; McAdoo, 1985; McNeil, 1999; Murray, Stokes, & Peacock, 1999; Rotherman & Phinney, 1987; Spencer, 1983; Spencer, Swanson, & Cunningham, 1991). According to Coard and colleagues (2004), racial socialization also refers to the promotion of psychological and physical health through childrearing in a society where dark skin and/or African features may lead to discrimination and racism, which in turn can lead to a host of detrimental outcomes for African Americans, such as high rates and chronicity of behavioral problems, depression, anxiety, and death (Peters, 1985). Stevenson, Herrero-Taylor, Cameron, and Davis (2002) contend that race-related socialization processes include divine, affective-symbolic, and phenomenological strategies that protect youth from discriminatory and psychological antagonistic environments; that mediate racism stress; and that are related to closer and more protective family relationships. Such traditional perspectives focus on most structures of socialization as being located within the family, but also as being seen located in centers of community outside the family, like barbershops and hair salons.

An investigation into the kinds of interaction patterns that occur in Kuttin' Up salon, for example, revealed a socialization orientation where the primary goal of participation in Shoptalk is the individual's application of certain strategies for solving life's dilemmas. As participants, youth were able to consider alternative perspectives, take on roles within the argumentation, and digest (and even assume) multiple points of view—skills that mimic those required in any language arts classroom. In Chapter 5, I report on an event in which those engaging in Shoptalk redirect the initial dilemma in nonthreatening ways and offer multiple perspectives from which to view that dilemma. As a result, the youth come to consider alternative perspectives and points of view.

NARRATIONS OF UNDERSTANDING

Before going any further, let's pause to consider the place of me, the researcher, in all of this. In qualitative research, the role of the researcher as the primary instrument of data collection necessitates the identification of researcher positioning within the research site (Cresswell, 2003). What this means is that in the field, "self" is a methodological, theoretical, and rhetorical instrument (Fine, 1994). My stance as a researcher and my ethnographic method for gathering data in the salon provided a space for new insights into the implications of appropriating community-based discourse structures and knowledge to support literacy within secondary language arts classrooms (Paredes, 1984).

In order to understand the complex processes of teaching and learning spaces that African Americans occupy, I invoked a kind of engagement, one that runs counter to or opposite from the traditional distanced stance many researchers take. Out of the traditional stance emerges a "narrative of the researched." This narrative of the researched is characterized by a view of objectivity and is manifested through a kind of distancing between the researcher and the researched subjects.

In educational research conducted in urban contexts, there is often a *gaze* that is enacted on the subject. This gaze leads to an ethnocentric assessment of what it means to teach and to learn. This gaze also lends itself to an overgeneralization of what it means to be a student, privileging a view of student as devoid of voice and ways of knowing that account for culture, context, community: all the things that make up a student. Research findings framed as narratives of the researched contribute to educational practices and discourses around achievement that reinscribe "particular behaviors, attitudes and performances" of teachers (Ladson-Billings, 2005, p. 115).

These attitudes, unfortunately, too often reward, sanction, and re-create a problematic understanding of what should be valued, as reflected in teachers' statements regarding the capacities of students. As Ladson-Billings argues, such discourses can create a blind spot for what it means to teach all students in teaching practice. This blind spot is exacerbated in classroom contexts (urban and suburban) that serve students of color, as it invokes a way of knowing grounded in misrepresentations, rather than experience. What is more, this narrative of the researched approach leads to the visibility of one voice—the teacher's or researcher's—while reproducing itself as that of the students. This voice becomes privileged, silencing all alternative ones. In the instance where the event involves an "Other," privilege dominates and voice and story are silenced from within, to make room for external acceptance of the Other by the privileged (Majors, 1998).

While narratives of researched can be characterized by a stance of objectivity and are manifested through an empirical distancing between the researcher and the researched subjects, *narratives of understanding* are quite the opposite. Narratives of understanding emerge not from the traditional gaze, but through a kind of grounded engagement. Grounded engagement is work that occurs in a unique space, somewhere between practitioner and researcher, teacher and learner, where one critically examines the meanings and functions of events held by all those who are involved in them (Fine, 1994). This examination leads to a multivoiced assessment of what it means to teach and to learn.

To be a researcher, teacher, or teacher educator from this perspective is to also be a student. Through grounded engagement the researcher/teacher is no longer the one who merely teaches, but rather she is the one who herself is taught in dialogue with the students, who in turn, while being taught, also teach (Majors, 1998). When resisting voice from a traditional gaze, we are resisting the Other and the maintenance of the the social and academic imbalances that social justice within education strives against. We also are enabling students to maintain the existing cultural hierarchy and imbalance of relevant talk and written expression. In taking up voice through engagement, we allow it to act as a vehicle by which students can navigate their understanding of the world in dialogue with the teacher.

Unlike the traditional narrative of the researched, which reflects the methods and actions of many of those in the field with regard to African American youth in schools, a narrative of understanding acknowledges the shared cultural landscape of the researched and the researcher. To gaze from this standpoint is to listen, perceive, and act on the ground, not separate from or in opposition to it. It is also to acknowledge participants' beliefs about what shapes, gives life to, and threatens their world and place within it.

TRANSFORMATIONS THROUGH MEANING-MAKING

For the uninitiated to bear witness to Shoptalk is in some ways similar to witnessing a flash mob in a train station. On the surface, the flash mob and Shoptalk discourse both appear to be spontaneous and sudden, perhaps even jolting if you are caught off guard. Yet, when you look long enough (but try not to stare), you see that each is a deliberate, well-coordinated act resulting in a text embedded with meaning.

Let me explain. In instances of a flash mob and of Shoptalk, participants display a kind of belonging owing to an awareness of shared space, time, tools, and purpose within each context. As Muse (2010) points out, their outward appearance would suggest that each person is suited to membership (role/part) in that community, which is constituted by not just the site, but the norms, goals, and tools that define these sites. In the description below, for example, a New York–based group, "Improv Everywhere," disrupts a busy afternoon commute with one of their most famous performances.

> At precisely 2:30 P.M. on a Saturday afternoon in 2006, more than 200 New Yorkers inexplicably froze in place on the main concourse of Grand Central Terminal, as if struck by a mysterious virus. Their apparel and positions suggested they were commuters whose daily rounds had come to an abrupt halt. One man was stuck checking his watch, which unlike him continued to move. Another was kneeling to pick up some papers that had spilled from his briefcase. Two lovers remained locked in a kiss as if in rebuke to Keats's vase. Around them, hundreds of other visitors struggled to comprehend this epidemic of stillness in one of the world's busiest places. Amazingly, much of the crowd continued walking. But others stopped and took note or wandered around the rigid bodies to inspect them.

This flash-mob performance illuminates this book's view of the actions of those engaged in Shoptalk. Both the flash mob and participants of Shoptalk *transform* space for the purpose of enacting *a role* and constructing and or suspending *an identity* and conveying *a message*. According to Muse (2010), flash mobs "follow a relatively schematic scenario" (p. 10), in which a group of apparently ordinary commuters gathers in a public space and suddenly bursts into a coordinated performance for a few moments, only to resume what we might anticipate are their ordinary activities. The same can be said for the participants of Shoptalk, in that ordinary people gather together in a space that functions dually as an interactional, commercial establishment where goods and services are provided on demand, and a distinct ritual setting, discourse being a part of that ritual.

In situated activity, like a flash mob and talk in the salon, both the individual and the social environment of which he or she is a participant *transform* through practice with and appropriation of cultural tools, the interpretation of those tools, and the resources of language and skills (Wells, 2000). The cultural and social resources that constitute transformations within the hair salon include linguistic and nonlinguistic ways of speaking, performing, and reasoning; culturally shared interactional norms; structures of argumentation; and engagement in problem solving.

Social Disruptions and the Construction of Social Texts

As in the case of the flash mob, the disruption of space alters the way the audience interacts. "Flash mobs are revolts against predictability," suggests Muse (2010, p. 21). In other words, they aim to disrupt some set of social circumstances and expectations. Similarly, in the salon there is a disruption that leads to a discursive revolt against predictability and expectation, imposed by a broader society regarding the identities, resilience, and capacities of the African American participants as human beings. Such disruptions of the old, in service of the new, take on structural significance for teaching and learning. These disruptions become a kind of text, a social text—the multi-voiced, multiscripted texts that convey, guide, inform, and generate meanings for learners, who simultaneously re-create and transform old understandings into the new, where they inscribe their readings of social relations.

Social Texts and Social Reading

People read social relations every day in daily life: the African American woman who waits at the checkout counter in the local grocery while the young White male checker meticulously scrutinizes her photo identification; the Mexican middle schooler, who nervously explains to his teacher that his mother is not sure how to help him with his homework; the elderly Korean woman who, while carrying groceries, hurriedly crosses the street as a group of young Black men approaches. Each of these people reads culture, class, gender, generation, and other relations, and acts on the world based on their readings of these social texts.

To *read* a social text, in the sense of understanding it, is to go beyond interpretation. It is to reconstruct, or rather rig, that text in action and consciousness, "to imitate it in some way, to produce something around it that is new but that bears some clear relationship to the original text" (Rabinowitz, 1987, p. 15). Understanding of social relations, as a kind of social text, is manifested in restating that text and in making those restatements public (Rabinowitz, 1987). When such readings are made public, social texts become one aspect of a complex psychological landscape of action and consciousness, and often are represented through narrative (Bruner, 1990). Thus, it may be argued that such readings of social relations are tools of literacy (and, in many cases, of survival) that call on skills of revising, improvising, recounting, inferencing, and making and fathoming the social and moral meanings of events (Ochs & Capps, 2001). They are part of the psychological (Wertsch, 1985), communal (Bruner, 1990), cultural (Swidler, 2001), and linguistic (Moll, 2000) toolkits that all individuals draw upon to reason through problem-solving activities.

The portion of dialogue presented earlier in this chapter between Ms. Addie and the others reflects their narrated social readings of the world and attempt to forge their own identities, ideologies, and problem-solving strategies in the context of cross-cultural interactions. Like functional reading, the social reading of narrative texts involves many and varied skills depending on the orientation of the task. Recall process, product, and socialization, discussed earlier. Yet unlike functional reading, social reading draws heavily on the skill of conversational inferencing (Gumperz, 1996). One indirectly or implicitly illustrates an understanding (reading) of what is said (oral narrative text) through verbal and nonverbal responses by the way one builds on (narrates) what one hears (reads). Reading of oral texts is integrally bound to notions of culture, class, and social relations. In the hair salon, the social reading of culture, class, and social relations in narrative texts is not only a skill that occurs within this context, but also a tool of skilled, practical/life problem solving. However, it is not the only skill. Human reality is very complex and is therefore not reducible to single, analytic domains (Rose, 2001). Although discourse is one of the many domains that contribute to what it means to know in the salon, there are others that are certainly worth exploring. For example, the expression of values, technical labor, the development of manual skill over time, as well as the work of memory in skill all contribute to the structure of the hair salon as a learning environment (Agre, 1997; Anyon, 1980; Brown & Duguid, 1991; Hutchins, 1996; Luff, Hindmarsh, & Heath, 2000; Orr, 1990, 1996; Rose, 2001, 2004).

The skills of social reading are likely to be displayed only in context-appropriate ways. They may be performed most dramatically and openly in situations in which the author/speaker feels confident that her audience will share her reading. Other situations may elicit much more cautious, tentative, or seemingly neutral social readings—but it is the very cautiousness, tentativeness, and neutrality of these readings that reveal the speaker's capacity to read and write appropriately for an unknown audience.

Individuals' constructions and readings of day-to-day events are constituted and narrated through talk in the hair salon, talk that reflects participants' racialized, gendered, and social class positionings. The narration of personal experience is an important piece to emphasize. In the context of the African American hair salon, narrative plays a significant role in framing and creating context and unveiling positionings of social actors, while simultaneously unveiling the ideologies and institutional assumptions inherent in those positionings. Miller et al. (1990) give us a sense of this when they argue, "When a person encounters another person, he or she projects a definition of the situation and thereby makes implicit or explicit claims to be a certain kind of person. . . . The self, as performed character, emerges as a byproduct of the interactive processes" (p. 295).

Arguably, all people engage in this kind of reading of social texts, where the local events are viewed against a backdrop of socially and culturally constructed meanings. However, the literate skills of reading the social relations embedded within these texts may be heightened for members of socially, economically, and academically under-represented cultures, who simultaneously and historically have been denied societal power, yet must navigate across institutions and interface daily with groups who hold and exercise such power. Skills are more than one's ability to read and to write. They are the institutional and cultural technology of intellectual activity (Rogoff, 1995), cultivated in particular cultural and linguistic contexts. Undergirding this particular skill of reading social text, I believe, is the ability to frame situations in domain-specific ways, that is, as social narrative (Ochs & Capps, 2001).

Within both the salon and classroom, readings of the world are socially constructed. Narrative text is part and parcel of how individuals make sense of word and world. This process or reading bridges action and consciousness in culturally and linguistically appropriate ways that involve skills that are important to domain-specific teaching and learning (e.g., secondary language arts). In culturally and politically constructed contexts (like beauty salons, barbershops, and classrooms), people read, write, talk, and think about real ideas and information in order to ponder and extend what they know, communicate with others, present their points of view, understand, and be understood (Langer, 1987). Reading within cultural and linguistic contexts involves an active evaluation of actions by protagonists, whose actions, thoughts, and feelings are interpreted in light of local notions of what is right and wrong, just and unjust.

Cultural Border Crossers' Readings of Culture, Class, and Social Relations

In the following chapters we will see how participants of discourse in the salon read one another's narrations of personal experience as a way of complex problem solving. Such reading is a literacy skill that adult and adolescent *cultural border crossers* rehearse and develop through their participation within specific, socially contingent discourses and/or through their movement across different kinds of discourse communities. I use the term *cultural border crosser* for people who actively move across the socially, culturally, and politically constructed and imposed divides (borders) that help to distinguish cultural groups/discourse communities one from another (Majors & Orellana, 2003). While all people move across social boundaries,

I distinguish cultural, linguistic, and social borders from social boundaries, as do Phelan, Davidson, and Cao Yu (1998):

> Borders are features of cultural difference that are not politically neutral. Boundaries are transformed into borders when the knowledge, skills and behaviors in one world are more highly valued and rewarded than those in another. . . . When boundaries exist (even when sociocultural components of [students'] worlds are different), movement between worlds can occur with relative ease—that is, social, psychological, and academic costs are minimal. Alternatively, when students encounter borders, movement and adaptation are difficult because knowledge and skills or particular ways of behaving in one world are more highly valued and esteemed than those in another. Although it is possible for students to navigate borders with apparent success, these transitions can incur personal and psychic costs invisible to teachers and others. (p. 10)

Analysis of cultural border crossings in relation to African American language use is significant and especially illuminating, particularly as African American verbal norms and cultural repertoires of practice continue to flourish "in spite of American middle class values which both criticize and fetishize the culture and language" (Morgan, 1998, p. 251). The result of this dualism "is a dominant culture which describes African American speech as bad, uneducated, unintelligible, etc., while wantonly imitating and celebrating its wit, creative vitality, and resilience" (p. 251). Such analysis provides a unique response to that duality by members of a nondominant culture who exercise their power in their own terms and language. Furthermore, it is the experience of talking among peers through these cross-cultural encounters that contributes to participants' shared repertoires of practice, where they draw on language to illuminate the meanings of these dualities, which they and their children must negotiate daily.

While others have focused on the border-crossing experiences of adolescents who negotiate family life, peer interactions, and school, I consider here the kind of border crossing that happens across the life span as people negotiate a range of cross-cultural encounters. Specifically, I explore culturally situated and literate skills used for crossing borders of culture, class, and language that include, but are not limited to, an awareness of norms and rhetorical structures, inferencing, improvisation, and signification (Booth, 1974; Lee, 1992; Rabinowitz, 1987).

In the following chapters I report on a kind of social reading of individuals' border-crossing experience drawn from the larger corpus of data. The analysis of the narrations closely examines the participants' (as social actors) use of linguistic and cultural tools as instruments for (1) problem

solving, (2) representing canonical relationships and values, and (3) interpreting and reading social texts. From this analysis I argue that:

- People positioned on the borders between cultural groups/discourse
  communities use cultural tools for reading social relations.
- Narrations of these readings can reveal their skills as readers and
  writers of social texts.
- People read social texts in different ways, through different affordances, with varying degrees of skill, linguistic norms, and
  traditions.
- The reading of power relations within and across cultural, linguistic,
  and gendered communities can serve as an important survival skill.

DIALOGIC REASONING WITHIN SHOPTALK

Part of the focus of my work is the application of a dialogic mode of problem solving (Kuhn & Crowell, 2011) through complex argumentative reasoning within the everyday setting of the salon and across to the classroom.

Unlike standard argument, where two sides listen to and respond to each
other and where the conclusions or outcomes may or may not be known
in advance, the situated discourse of Shoptalk reveals a complex line process
that is inherent in the culturally situated, *dialogically structured arguments*—
multivoiced responses to a proposition that has been posed and interpreted in
light of opposing systems of values and propositions of power. As Figure 2.4 illustrates, unlike the typical linearity inherent in standard structure of argumentation (where there is a presentation of a single proposition or claim followed
by grounds, warrants, and backing, leading to a single, expected conclusion or
outcome), the structure of argument within Shoptalk is highly dynamic.

In addition to taking on roles within the discourse, participants can
take one of two approaches. The first involves an official claim and the
explicit "guidance" of some group member by other, more knowledgeable
members of the group who, through deliberate attempts, draw on cultural
materials and experiences in order to instruct, encourage, and influence the
direction in which they wish that individual to go or not go (Rogoff, 1995).
The second approach entails less explicit guidance, involves multiple unofficial claims, is stronger in tone and pitch, and sounds like an overlapping,
multipartied, and collaborative debate, where there is no clear designated
expert. Hence, skilled, culturally situated dialogic arguments in this context appeal to more than commonsense notions or "gossip." Rather, this
structure appeals to thoughtful analysis of multiple possibilities and frames

Figure 2.4. Shoptalk Dialogic Argumentation Structure

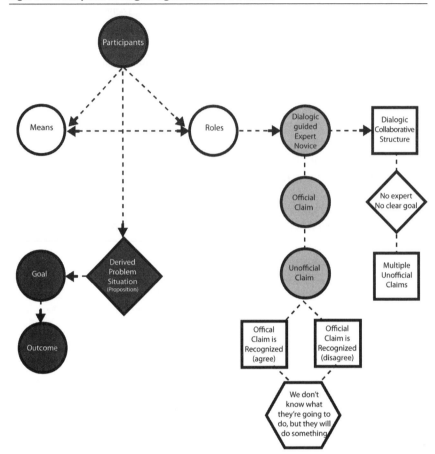

intergenerational beliefs, values, and traditions for African American children and the reproduction of ideologies within a protected safe space.

Culturally situated dialogic arguments in the salon have both interior
(argument as product) and exterior (argument as process) elements and take
the form of a kind of collaborative narrative text, where those involved formulate a line of reasoning to refute a particular claim, while simultaneously
establishing another, or counter, claim. A key aspect of this line of reasoning
within argument is individuals taking up alternative perspectives as they
move through the process of transformation.

For example, when participants of Shoptalk introduce new evidence to
the holder of an official claim, he or she is able to integrate such evidence
into this implicit weighing process. Each new piece of evidence does not
dominate or destroy a reasoned argument, however. Hence, any reasoned

argument in support of an assertion implicitly contains a full *dialogic argument* (Kuhn, 1991, 2005, 2015; Kuhn & Crowell, 2011). The cultural and linguistic factors that underlie dialogic argumentation can be observed and documented. Such documentation reveals not only the skilled reasoning practices of the participants, but also the deep connection between social and mental activity. There are several implications here:

- This identity between arguments in their rhetorical and dialogic forms makes it feasible to examine people's mastery of argumentative reasoning skills without asking them to engage in dialogic arguments.
- Dialogic argumentation offers a framework for examining the nature of the less externally observable rhetorical argument and its role in thinking.
- Goal directed, collaborative problem solving
- Competent argumentative discourse requires the ability to reflect on one's own thinking as an object of thought as well as the ability to interact with, examine, and represent multiple perspectives (Kuhn, 2015).

Narrative

The use of narrative within these culturally situated, dialogic arguments serves a couple of purposes. First, it contributes to a group dynamic by way of engagement through culturally normed (tempo, drum, rhythmic) responses (call and response). There is more than one narrator, as each member of the participation structure provides paralinguistic and linguistic supports to other participants. At the same time, however, narrative contributes to contested individual and group positionings within the argumentation. Second, narratives in this context are tied to the ways in which participants critique human action. Participants use narrative as a vehicle by which to take an ethical stance and to make meaningful their experiences (as individuals) and the experiences of others in support of claims, namely, by understanding themselves and their positions rationally.

Narrative is one way through which individuals represent their understandings of social relations and the interplay that takes place between external actions and internal consciousness (Bruner, 1990). As an aspect of cultural communication in African American communities, narrative is intimately tied to the cultural-communal-psychological toolkit of individuals. The process of constructing narrative within Shoptalk is an act of resistance to what Derrick Bell (1995) has termed *interest convergence*—"people believe what benefits them" (p. 22).

In Shoptalk, narratives provide a language to bridge the gaps in imagination and conception that give rise to certain cross-cultural conflicts regarding group perceptions of concepts such as justice and education. They reduce alienation for participants of Shoptalk, as members of excluded groups, while offering opportunities for members of the majority group to meet them halfway. Cultural narrative practices become a resource to the extent that the individual resists, accedes to, seizes upon, or in some way makes use of the self-relevant messages embodied therein. Narratives produced within Shoptalk provide a foundation from which to view the dialogic quality of voice in the hair salon and classroom. Dialogicality precedes both utterance and voice (Bakhtin, 1986). The utterance is filled with dialogic overtones that include the dialogic orientation between the utterances of one person and the utterances of another (Wertsch, 1993). Hence, in Shoptalk, dialogic harmony is achieved and viewed throughout the rendering of the entire narrative and through the responses of the audience to the speaker.

Likewise, counter-narratives produced within Shoptalk invoke narrative knowledge and storytelling *to challenge the social construction of identity, race, and power*, eschewing the experiences of White, European Americans as the normative standard, and grounding its conceptual framework, instead, in the distinctive contextual experiences of people of color. Within Shoptalk, counter-narrative functions as a resource by which individuals are able to resist dominant discourse, while at the same time giving voice to racial injury.

Both narrative and counter-narrative enable individuals to represent their understandings of social relations and the interplay that takes place between external actions and internal consciousness. As an aspect of cultural communication in AAE-dominant contexts, counter narrative is intimately tied to the cultural-communal-psychological toolkit of individuals.

Narratives and counter-narratives jointly produced in Shoptalk:

- Afford alternative perspectives
- Evoke personal and collective narratives of border crossing
- Open a window onto ignored or alternative realities, scripts, and narratives
- Challenge the social construction of identity, race, and power, eschewing the experiences of White, European Americans as the normative standard

The Skills of Shoptalk Argument

Within Shoptalk, the connection between the social and the internal, the individual and the community, lies in the connection between dialogic and rhetorical narrative argument structures. Both entail a skillful weighing of evidence, and it is this weighing process that is implicit when we speak of reasoned arguments. These skills include, but may not be limited to, the ability to:

- Identify the underlying meaning or intent of an utterance
- Understand the position of the speaker as it shapes authorial intent
- Identify implied audience
- Mutually understand and engage in Black modes of discourse
- Make paralinguistic, prosodic, gestural, code, and lexical choices
- Identify and evoke roles within interactions
- Enact an epistemic stance through the use of scripts
- Engage the Other's claims with the goal of redirecting those claims in light of alternative perspectives
- Attend to cultural norms that frame the discourse, such as multi-party, overlapping talk
- Step in and claim the floor
- Advance arguments that are supported by narrative and that strengthen one's own position
- Tacitly coordinate argument strategies with other speakers

A sociocultural view of Shoptalk, therefore, conceptualizes both informal and formal learning environments as sites of negotiation and co-constructed knowledge. It invites the design of instructional conversations that enables individuals to enact their roles as problem-solvers from a critical standpoint and draws on community-based norms for talk and problem solving as the medium for the generation of coping strategies that are hybrid in nature. It also attempts to account for other forms of social interaction, like argumentation, that entail and account for divergent perspectives, opposition of ideas, resistance to communication, and other disharmonious episodes that often are found within the discourse and should not be viewed simply as failed attempts at intersubjectivity. Shoptalk, in the classroom and hair salon, therefore, offers us a way to externalize the internal thinking strategies that many individuals engage in.

The following chapter will explore the nature of work practice in the African American salon as viewed by participants. In particular, we will identify some of the things that characterize what individuals do within that practice, what skills they account for in doing it, and the institutional principles (curriculum) that are intended as a general rule of action for accomplishing institutional goals. By examining how individuals across several African American hair salons make use of the cultural-institutional aspects of the event, which constitute activity within practice, we may better understand how learning takes place in this informal, out-of-school environment. Furthermore, identifying the instructional potential of a community hair salon might serve to "facilitate strategic connections" (Moll, 2000, p. 360) across other communities of practice, most specifically the classroom.

The process of problem solving among employees involves both collaborative sense making and narrative improvisation. Specifically, a focus on novice employees shows them as readers of narrative texts who must dialogically probe alternative, sometimes conflicting, versions of what has or could have transpired and attempt to piece together alternative perspectives. Novice readings of narrative texts call for openness to contingency, improvisation, and revision, and often result in the emergence of something new, rigged from its original—again, features that have import for classroom settings.

CHAPTER 3

Institutional Organization of Community Practice

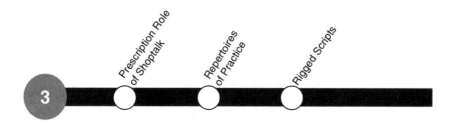

How are teaching and learning viewed in the context of the salon and what can that teach us?

Work is a socially valued, income-generating activity where people take on roles for the purposes of producing specific outcomes, such as providing goods or needed services. Work is a target institution of other institutions, like schools, that arguably prepare and develop individuals in order that they may perform optimally within a professional work environment. Work is also a popular topic of conversation within many social settings.

In the salon, for example, people talk about issues related to both their personal and professional lives. Conversations within and about work occupy a great deal of time and verbal space, as they offer participants occasions for small talk ("Sure was a long commute today"), big talk devoted to events within popular media/culture ("So I hear that new mayor is planning on closing down 10 more schools on the South Side"), to even bigger, closer to home talk deriving from personal events ("You know, I've been on that job 20 years, have trained at least 10 bosses, and they still saying I ain't done enough to be a manager").

In each of these instances, people are engaging in talk as they grapple with particular topics, issues, and dilemmas. Chances are that over the course of the conversation individuals develop some kind of knowledge and/or coping strategy that could inform similar performances or a shifting in attitude down the road. However, while talk around the topic of work is useful, for our purposes it does not provide a full understanding of the relationship that exists between work, learning, and language. Missing is what we can discover through an examination of what people do while they work, and their processes of preparation to do it (Scribner, 1984).

In this chapter we will get a glimpse into *what* participants view as key work tasks and skills for accomplishing the institutional goals. We also will get a sense of *how* they believe such work tasks are and/or should be performed to meet institutional expectations. We will get a glimpse into how participation in Shoptalk influences processes for the kinds of strategies associated with those tasks. The questions we want to ask are:

- What are the community's values and beliefs about the skills and characteristics contributing to individuals' occupational success within that particular community context?
- What tools are people expected to apply in order to accomplish particular goals and tasks and where do these tools come from?
- Do institutional expectations always align with actual individual performance?
- How do expectations and performance of these relate to the broader external community?

My observations of (and engagement in) certain occupational practices in the salon give us access to the beliefs, skills, values, understandings, and renditions of concepts of several key participants. Each participant takes on one or more occupational role, including expert stylist, apprentice stylist, stylist's assistant, administrative "front-end" staffer, and management/ owner. Additionally, each employer or employee holds some kind of status within the discourse, which, as we will see, contributes to the characterization of Shoptalk as a discourse of culturally shared technical and professional expertise.

A CERTAIN KIND OF EMPLOYEE

Given the general role that work plays in the human life span, the Black hair salon, as an economic, social, and historical institution, provides a situated context from which we can examine *what adults do* on the job and the structures, resources, tools, and processes involved in *how they do it* (Agre, 1997; Breier, 2005; Dirkx, 1996). It also provides a useful context from which to explore, from a historical and sociological standpoint, the nature of the evolving socioeconomic and macroeconomic systems that contribute to that community and the shifts and changes therein (Orr, 1996). In their studies of work within technical firms, Barley and Orr (1997) argue that "institutions [like schools] cannot effectively reorganize or re-engineer operations [like the curriculum] without understanding the work that its employees [like students] do" (p. 5). Studies have shown, however, that employers in most institutions, and those who utilize and depend on them, do not understand the work of their employees (Dirkx, 1996). Furthermore, contradictions, mismatches, and misunderstandings abound when it comes to connecting the outcomes of work to the actual practices of the employees that facilitated those outcomes.

As in schools, workplace practices are nuanced and at times can be difficult to observe and discern as either relevant or counterproductive to the accomplishment of the task itself. As a result, what ends up being evaluated, and ultimately held in high or low regard, may in fact omit or take for granted the kinds of resources and tools that contribute to the outcomes; for example, beliefs, skills, values, incomplete understandings, false beliefs, and the naïve renditions of concepts that newcomers bring with them to a given subject or task in a new situation.

Let's peek over at Darlene, lead stylist and owner of PA hair salon, located in a small, midwestern town, and Angela, Darlene's apprentice. Darlene is a self-described African American "hair technician" whose role within the salon is that of owner/manager/"master stylist," and whose status within the participation framework of the discourse of Shoptalk is that of "animator"—the one who renders the voice of the narrative (Duranti, 1997, p. 297). Angela, a young White woman and newcomer to the salon, is a recent hair school graduate and apprentice stylist. Angela's status within the participation framework of the discourse of Shoptalk is interesting and will be discussed further in this chapter. Most interesting with regard to Angela, however, is the role that Darlene attributes to her as an employee of the salon, one that goes beyond that of apprentice.

For example, in the excerpt below, Darlene explains to me her reasoning behind Angela's hire.

> *Darlene:* See . . . I'm gone put it to you like this. When I go over to the schools, and I do my training sessions and I teach, I pay close attention to anyone there that could provide for me an exoticness, an eroticness, or somethin different . . .
> *Yolanda:* So to you Angela is exotic?
> *Darlene:* Yeah, exactly. She was when I saw her and she provided for me a challenge.
> *Yolanda:* What do you mean by exotic?

Darlene: She's exotic in the sense of the word that we are in Iowa in the middle of a corn-fed state. She was the first Caucasian I've met that had an interest in ethnic hair, and had no fear.

Yolanda: Of the repercussions?

Darlene: Exactly. To me that is somewhat unusual. In the sense that it does make it an exotic thing. It's no different than me being thrust into the middle of openings and to sit on a women's panel of art and being the only Black person in 1,500. For them I'm exotic.

Yolanda: At the same time, though, I was ashamed because that was the same way that I thought of it. I thought, I said that I am exoticizing this person but I hate it when I'm exoticized.

Darlene: (laughs) But she is. There's no way, there's no way around it. There's no way around it. But when I started to work with Angela, I told her that what would happen is that there would be a lot of resistance. But because of the fact that I was the one introducing her into the shop, my clients . . .

Yolanda: Would respect her?

Darlene: Would respect her.

Yolanda: So Tanya, how do you feel about that exoticism?

Tanya: I don't know. I don't think about it 'cause . . .

Darlene: 'Cause Angela is just a person to you?

Tanya: Um hm.

In the above excerpt, Darlene uses the term *exotic* in describing not only Angela's ethnic identity, but also her fearless disposition toward working with Black hair. According to Darlene, it was Angela's fearlessness that made her stand out from the crowd. For Darlene, Angela's disposition is important in an apprentice inasmuch as it contributes to the enactment of the overall vision she has for her business.

Darlene: I always look at everything from the total spectrum. And everything that I do, I have an ulterior motive for doing it. And when I went in to train Angela I had an ulterior motive for doing it. And my ulterior motive came from this. I went to Ames, Iowa, to get my hair done. Walked in the shop and there was, it was a White shop that had Aveda products, that's the reason I selected the shop 'cause I knew that I could get the oils and moisture back into my hair. So I walked in and I wanted them to blow dry and curl me. Now, these people couldn't do that for me. They could not do it for me and it angered me. I sent my husband in [who is White] and they gave him a haircut. But they said that they didn't have anyone that could do a blow dry, a shampoo/blow dry.

Yolanda: Is there a difference between a shampoo/blow dry for a Black person and a shampoo/blow dry for a White person?

Darlene: No, but they thought so. They thought so. So nobody would take the time to do my hair because they were afraid to do my hair. So my thang is when I start training and teaching, I wouldn't have even ever started to train or teach a stylist that can't do everybody's hair. Except for the fact that when I start trainin' or teachin' 'em, I start doin' that because I wanted to erase that division line.

Yolanda: That fear of Otherness?

Darlene: Exactly. And I do the same thang for Black stylists workin' with Caucasian hair.

The above excerpt speaks to an appropriation of the stylist's role in the salon as one aspect of the institutional organization of community practices. According to Darlene, fear and Otherness are the dividing lines that differentiated what she envisioned for her salon and her employees from those of others, particularly those who denied her service based on her identity as a Black woman. From Darlene's perspective, it is the work of the institution to blur such lines, and the role of the stylist, as "fearless" if not "exotic," to facilitate that.

Such a perspective illuminates how, for members of this community, specialization of roles is oriented toward the accomplishment of a broad, often nuanced, set of goals. These institutional roles distinguish Darlene and her stylists from those outside of their community and involve Darlene as expert and architect of PA's vision and goals. Angela, whose roles include "exotic" resource, is also a learner—someone who is being scaffolded into the community culture, while developing skill and understanding in the process of performing particular and nuanced tasks and institutional goals. This is relevant, as such a dynamic goes "far beyond expert–novice dyads" that often are used to characterize teacher and student engagements and arrangements (Rogoff, 1995). Rather, it directs our attention to a complex system of teaching and learning—a system where people are deeply engaged in culturally and socially defined and organized ways. A broad, complex network of external social paradigms, scripts, and social factors, such as race, class, and gender, influences such engagement.

As an "expert" stylist, Darlene illuminates the view of Shoptalk as a discourse of technical and professional expertise by constructing several interrelated identities or roles for herself within the salon—teacher, stylist, medical expert, and analyst (see Jacobs-Huey, 1996, 1997a, 1997b for a more extensive discussion of this view):

We as stylists actually become almost like psychiatrists because you work so closely with [clients] and because you are responsible for their outer image they reveal their inner selves to you. And for me, I manipulate the clients to get them to do that because I need to know who they are on the inside and therefore I can create a look for them on the outside. And that's the whole teaching experience. That's what I'm trying to get the girls to learn. . . . And when you're talkin' to your client, you don't need to tell them about your personal life. You don't need to be hearin' about Judy down the street. The only thing that you need to be talkin' to them about is them. And there has to be a way that you get focused into their life enough that you become very concerned about that person in that chair and that person only.

To account for the role of the stylist in interaction with clients, Darlene appropriates the expert medical term *psychiatrist*. In so doing, she constructs an expert knowledge not only of the responsibility of stylists in general, but of the identity and needs of all clients. Further, Darlene unpacks this medical identity early on, suggesting that she "manipulates the clients" to prompt them to share their inner views of themselves.

This makes explicit not only the analogous relation between beauty expert and medical expert, but the shifting from one to the other and back again. Furthermore, through her construction of this identity, Darlene enacts an epistemic, knowing stance in order to construct her own expert knowledge by evoking scripts (Gutierrez, Rymes, & Larson, 1995; Jacobs-Huey, 1997b; Schank & Abelson, 1977), the common everyday phenomena of what people—in this case, doctors—do. It is this expert knowledge that leads Darlene to the construction of a second identity, that of teacher. Here Darlene appropriates the role of teacher, asserting herself as "trying to get the girls to learn."

The term *girls* refers to Angela and the additional hair stylist in the salon, Tanya. This term also contributes to the construction of a paradigm that asserts a community hierarchy of power and knowledge within the salon. Within this paradigm, power and knowledge become tools that separate and distinguish occupational roles, the performance of certain tasks, as well as overall outcomes. This paradigm also separates Darlene not only from the clients but from the other stylists as well, who lack the knowledge to elicit and apply understanding of clients' self-views. Finally, this paradigm of power and knowledge contributes to the overlapping of identities in which Darlene is expert psychiatrist and teacher, dominant to both clients and girls. Darlene asserts expertise not only in psychiatric methodologies, but in the use of these methods as a part of her instruction.

There are a couple of things that are particularly interesting about Darlene's perspective. The first has to do with the deliberate and purposeful partnering between practice and talk in PA salon. Hairstyling is the trademark practice within Darlene's salon, and talk is the expert practitioner's tool. It is at the intersection of these that we gain access to the connective tissues that join precepts and practice (Brown & Duguid, 1991), which is action. Within that context, the principle intended as the general rule is what governs stylists' actions and, at least for Darlene, puts practice into motion.

Given the emphasis that Darlene places on talk, it would be easy for us to assume that it, along with hairstyling, is the intended action. However, as Darlene points out, talk serves as a vehicle for her goal, one that is more nuanced and less visible, which is the matching of clients' internal profiles to an external look. The application of this principle, the connective tissue between talk and hairstyling, is the prescriptive role of Shoptalk.

Within Shoptalk, participants hold status as speakers and hearers. Shoptalk allows stylists to both engage with their clients and match hairstyles to their clients' psychological (thus cognitive) needs. This hair "talkin'" is an analysis capable of being made only by the stylist (as a beauty/psychology expert) of the client. For Darlene, this complex construction of the stylist with the interrelated identities of beauty and analytical expertise was to the client's benefit and ultimately the driving force of her actions—styling hair.

Darlene's declaration of creating a look for clients is also very interesting, as it locates for us at least one problem-solving task within the activity structure, which is, how do you create an external look for someone through developing internal understanding? This not only opens up a door for considering the kinds of assumptions that people make as they are attempting to "know" someone on the inside in order to match that to the outside, but it also leads us to some really complex questions—How do you go from the inside to the outside in this context? Is talk the only and most appropriate vehicle? What other things do you need to consider, both with regard to the individual and to certain values and social, cultural, gendered positionings that they may or may not hold? Is there an automatic straight line from the inside of a person to the outside? The answer to the last question is, No, there is not. In other words, just because Darlene "observes" something about a person's disposition, personality, circumstances, or history does not automatically mean there's a direct and straight line to what the outside image should be. For example, in order for Darlene to come to the kinds of aesthetic conclusions that she draws through talk, she also must be reading other socially constructed factors that do not exist inside any person, such as mainstream standards of beauty.

"I DON'T REALLY TALK THAT MUCH":
COMPETING PATHWAYS IN SOCIAL PRACTICE

Let's take a closer look now at Angela. In institutions like schools, evaluations and assessments are grounded in a set of expectations derived from certain practices and the resulting outcomes of those practices. Teachers and employers can build on what new members bring to new tasks embedded in the institution's practices in ways meant to help each new member develop and achieve a more mature understanding of the task. However, if new members' cultural tools, initial beliefs, and existing skills are ignored, the understanding that they develop can be very different from what the community expects, resulting in kinds of tensions, conflicts, and resolutions within the task that lend themselves to learning. The general view of learning, in recent years, has been that people construct new knowledge and understanding through interactions with others and based on what they already know (Piaget, 1926; Vygotsky, 1978). In other words, each of us comes to new social, cultural, and institutional circumstances, be it at work or in school, with a range of skills, practices, beliefs, concepts, and values that significantly influence what we notice about the situation and how we organize and interpret what we encounter. This in turn affects how we interpret and reason through tasks, problem-solve, and acquire new knowledge within this new context (Bransford, Brown, & Cocking, 2000).

Hair stylists, like all human beings, occupy membership in a multitude of communities. However, no matter what community a particular individual stylist identifies with, occupationally they could all have the same goal—reading the inside of a person to figure out what they really need on the outside. But the path to what the outside is, however, will be dramatically influenced by external social and cultural values as well as how those values match up with the individual's values. For example, in addition to Darlene, there is an audience of clients within PA salon whose status is considered ratified participants of the talk. Ratified, or accepted, participants of Shoptalk take on the role of cultural border crosser, as they actively move across the socially, culturally, and politically constructed and imposed divides (borders) that help to distinguish cultural groups/discourse communities one from another.

As noted earlier, borders are features of cultural difference that are not politically neutral. Boundaries are transformed into borders when the knowledge, skills, and behaviors in one world are more highly valued and rewarded than those in another. When boundaries exist, even when, for example, sociocultural components of students' worlds are different, movement between worlds can occur with relative ease—that is, social, psychological, and academic costs are minimal. Alternatively, when students encounter borders, movement and adaptation are difficult because knowledge and skills or particular ways of behaving in one world are more highly valued and esteemed than those in another. Although it is possible for students to navigate borders with apparent success, these transitions can incur personal and psychic costs invisible to teachers and employers.

Within Shoptalk, ratified participants are entitled and expected to be a part of the communicative event. Unratified participants are not. In PA salon, Angela is viewed by clients and coworkers as a White female hair stylist who "doesn't talk much 'cause she's White," as one client stated. My own analysis of discourse events when Angela was present revealed her resistance to talking with clients. Such resistance shines a spotlight on the tensions that can occur when culturally situated and nuanced aspects of practice are deemed to be an inherent aspect of an individual and/or as deficient by members of the community. For Darlene, Shoptalk was one aspect of practice in that it functioned as a prescriptive mediational tool for getting things done. However, absent from Angela's occupational toolkit is a shared belief in the function and utility of Shoptalk. When I asked Angela how she regarded talk, she replied:

> I don't really talk much, and I don't know if people like that in me. . . . A lot of times they say your clients will come to you 'cause of your personality and not necessarily if you do their hair good or whatever. But I don't believe that. I think that people come to you to get their hair done, you know. And they want it done right. I do feel it slows me up to get in a conversation. . . . I don't like that at all.

Angela's belief is that the role of the technician or stylist is to do hair, and goals can be accomplished in the absence of institutionally valued tools, such as talk. According to Angela, this is what the client wants. As indicated above, "people come to you to get their hair done. . . . And they want it done right." While Darlene explicitly constructs several interrelated identities for herself, Angela on the other hand appears not to and views her role in the salon as that of stylist, not as one in which she must engage in conversational discourse that functions as a prescriptive tool or otherwise. This perspective is informed by an interwoven, complex set of social and cultural rules and standards for particular events that extend beyond the confines of the salon, moving across space and time, and informing how these stylists view their roles in these and similar events.

For various reasons (which include issues of time and efficiency), many individuals, both White and Black, share Angela's point of view concerning the relevancy of talk in the salon. However, Angela's expressed point of view might be characterized as demonstrating a kind of "restraint set by cultural standards for events in which expression is seen as having little or no functional role" (Kochman, 1981, p. 114). Important to note, however, is that Angela's approach to hairdressing is a characteristic she draws from participation in similar events where talk is not viewed as a necessity, and not because of some inherent ethnic trait. According to Gutierrez and Rogoff (2003), variations in practice "reside not as traits of individuals or collections of individuals, but as proclivities of people with certain histories of engagement with specific cultural activities" (p. 19). Hence, Angela's view is not a White one or a Black one. Rather, it is one that is drawn from her own repertoire of practice—"the ways of engaging in activities stemming from observing and otherwise participating in cultural practices" (p. 22). As the authors suggest, an important feature of focusing on repertoires, as opposed to some other trait such as race or ethnicity, is that it encourages people such as students to develop dexterity in determining which approach from the repertoire is appropriate under which circumstances (Rogoff, 2003).

Angela's perspective, and the resources she draws upon, deviates sharply from Darlene's, despite the fact that they would appear to be accomplishing similar tasks. Furthermore, because certain AAE discourse norms located in the talk between Darlene and her clients are not in (or evident within) Angela's linguistic and cultural repertoire, she may remain relatively passive and not engage in this cultural process (Gutierrez et al., 1995; Smitherman, 1977). This is also true regarding broader contexts that could include students within the classroom.

As "teacher," Darlene makes her expectations clear as to the kinds of practices that are tied to particular roles that she believes will ensure particular outcomes. As a "student," or rather one of "those girls," Angela does not appear to buy into such roles or tool use, which the teacher has deemed appropriate for the accomplishment of particular tasks. Hence, Angela's view is oppositional to her occupational role within the salon, despite the fact that she does manage to keep her job and maintain a modest African American client base. This tension between Darlene's expectations and Angela's deviation from them illuminates the very complicated issue of aligning precepts and principles when it comes to how we make sense of and evaluate the outcomes of work tasks with the actual practices and tools that facilitated them.

For Darlene, a stylist's success and failure are attributed to his or her foregrounding of the internal—one's ability to socially and psychologically get inside the heads of clients. Darlene's desire for a certain kind of employee, and her guiding principle—that one must be willing to psychologically probe the client's needs through the use of talk—are relevant. They reflect, in part, one expert's view of practice, the goals associated with that practice, and the means by which she believes such practices are accomplished. On the other hand, Angela's view is critically important as well. It sheds light on a tension that exists between Darlene's precepts and her own. This tension, a mismatch between views of the appropriation of a particular institutional tool, is not easily reconciled and has consequences for how each participant, teacher and student, takes up her respective institutional role, makes choices concerning appropriation of particular tools, and gets behind the attainment of the ultimate shared goal of profit.

A CERTAIN KIND OF CULTURE

Researchers have been very interested in how an appropriation of skills that fall into the very specific domains of mathematics, engineering, and technology contributes to work performance (Orr, 1990; Scribner, 1984). While important, such descriptions often fail to account for the nuances within the details of engaging in practice. For example, learning to "do" hair, learning to write a paper, learning to repair a broken furnace or busted carburetor, and learning to waitress—are all tasks that require both explicit instruction, individual deviation from that instruction, as well as how individuals account for that variation in changing conditions (e.g., doing "ethnic hair," writing a "research" paper, repairing a 1990 Whirlpool furnace). Furthermore, in spite of such nuances and varying circumstances, the standard operating plan (curriculum) of the workplace or the classroom may not account for (1) the variation that can occur within a problem-solving task; (2) the variation that exists between individual learners; and (3) apprenticeship processes and practices that are or are not transparent and align with institutional goals and desired outcomes.

John, co-owner and lead operator of Posh salon, complements Darlene's view of what it means to become successful within one's occupation and the means by which to do so in interesting ways. According to John, the most successful employee is one with a focus on physical appearances of self and client, with little emphasis on talk. John's official precept regarding apprenticeship is one where there is a foregrounding of external appearance and physical body as the most highly regarded tool of practice. What makes the best stylist stand out from the pack is neither talk nor deftness of hand, but rather his or her ability to aesthetically model a social ideal.

Located in the upscale section of a large, urban city in the southern region of the United States, the occupational goal of any stylist at Posh is explicit mastery of social form and image. The key tool, whose function is to ensure customer satisfaction and loyalty, is not talk, but rather appearance. In other words, it is the public image of the salon as an "exclusive," "high-end," and "industry-competitive" institution that's always foremost in John's mind and the employee is always viewed in relation to that image.

A close look into the institutional structure and kinds of interaction patterns that occurred in Posh salon revealed that the goals of work tasks were situated within a kind of *institutional curriculum* or *standard operating plan* of John. John's goal is one of institutional profit, achieved through the creation of a loyal customer base fostered by the culture of the salon and its employees. John's belief is that any business, particularly a small- to mid-sized one, needs to be "focused and work well together" in order to succeed. Thus, John works hard to create an institutional curriculum—from weekly meetings to strict standards on employees' appearance—that meets his goals.

This curriculum is evident in a variety of ways throughout the salon. For example, by using "multicultural" and high-end products in his salon like Aveda and Phyto—products that are not often distributed through "ethnic" neighborhood beauty supply shops or in the homes of working-class and/or low-income African American women—he maintains a certain sense of class stratification and money awareness within the salon, a sentiment he works to perpetuate. In other words, he purposely creates a sense of separation between the salon and the everyday home in an attempt to ignite within the client the "desire for something different, something better."

To further enhance the salon's image and instill a separation between what is offered outside of the salon and what is offered to clients inside, John, for example, also demands that clients receive the highest level of customer service. This, he believes, will ensure customer loyalty and more profit.

> I know the type of clientele we have; our clientele . . . 50% of 'em are wearing a great hairstyle, but 50% of 'em want customer service, an' if you can do a decent hairstyle with great customer service, you'll be successful. An' thas' like Aaron is a perfect example of it. I'm not saying he's not a, a good hairstylist, but his customer service excels on everybody else's. So when you have that customer service, your ability to maintain a client is . . . far beyond everybody else.

John believes that the affective response of clients to the salon's customer-service relations is even stronger than their appreciation of the hairstyling service. Thus, ultimately for John, the "product" of the salon is really customer service and image, not hairstyling. This is manifested in the curriculum of his all-staff meetings as well. One of the main issues addressed at one staff meeting was the dress code. Before this meeting, the dress code of the salon had been all black. However, he changed it so that the salon would have alternating weeks of black and khaki—one week would be all khaki, the next all black. Again, the point of change is not about hairstyling or technique, but about the image the salon is portraying and "working" that image. Arguably, this attempt to impose a kind a culture and image within the salon through separation and designation of certain practices creates and sustains isolation between individuals within that context. Ultimately, creating that culture becomes a game of hype, where the illusion of superiority (superiority not based on skill) outweighs the accomplishment of particular tasks.

To achieve this goal of the "desiring client," John strategically throws an institutional spark into occupational practices, in that he requires all of his employees, particularly the stylists, to be dressed in modern, high-end fashionable clothing, and to enter the salon red carpet style through the front door, maximizing face-time with clients and creating an association of the salon with glamour. In instituting such practices, not only is John creating a certain structural aesthetic (both in physical structure and employee appearance), but he is also ensuring an affective response of the clients to the salon. These markers of wealth in the salon tend to draw both a wealthy and desire-to-be-wealthy clientele. Hence, John manipulates the clients as Darlene reads the clients.

John's curriculum attempts to create a *certain kind of culture* within the salon and maintain a certain kind of employee.

> You put everybody on the same page an' everybody with the same goals, an' you can grow further, faster. And the, um, camaraderie and the, um, passion for everybody achieving the goals.

In addition to the use of aesthetic influences as tools, John desires the kind of worker that not only facilitates certain appearances, but also ensures customer loyalty for the good of the business, one that is high-quality and independent and able to readily meet the demands placed upon them. According to John, the best employee is one who is technically innovative and takes on their institutional role "already knowing exactly how to do everything in the salon." For example, John initiates the novice employee into the performance of work tasks on the busiest days in the salon. He states that this is to facilitate the goal of both accomplishing the work task and socializing novice employees into that task. In this process of initiation, however, John does not guide or scaffold the novice employee nor does he provide tools (e.g., manuals and orientations) for employees to accomplish work tasks. As a result, successful new employees are those who begin the job either already equipped with the skills needed or ones who are able to improvise alternate routes to success.

While John views himself as a nurturing and motivating employer, this belief sharply contrasts with a "sink-or-swim" approach that frames the salon's *stated* curriculum.

What I try to do is get the best I can get out of each individual. I mean, how can I utilize that individual . . . if I interview you, I wanna make sure that you're looking for some type of management responsibilities. . . . So, I need people who wanna grow, an' want more . . . my expectations, a lotta times are higher than people have of themselves.

John presents a kind of curriculum or standard operating plan here, one that aims to generate a profit and high levels of customer service. The underlying belief is that this ultimately leads to better employees. John's language in describing his efforts to implement what may be labeled an institutional "curriculum" reveals a stance toward employee performance on work-place tasks that is not necessarily in line with his actions. For example, John states that he looks for ways to "utilize" his employees and get the most out of them. In stating that he wants his employees to "look for some type of management responsibilities," John appears to aim for cutting out the middleman, which in turn places more pressure on individual workers to figure things out for themselves and deal with problems independently. This again shifts the responsibility of teaching and learning onto the employees and away from John.

John conveys the image he perceives of himself as a leader when he states that he believes his "expectations" are "higher than [those employees] have for themselves." This view, paired with his tough love style, creates a kind of black box in learning, where process and product are vaguely presented, lacking both transparency and form for the learner. Despite John's stated curriculum, ultimately the implied curriculum teaches that at the end of the day, the impression of successful task completion is much more important than the means by which it is accomplished. Thus, employees must rely on innovative ways to fulfill their job tasks. The absence of explicit instruction or scaffolding for novices can be potentially detrimental, as certain skills are never attained and workplace tasks may not be accomplished in the manner that John would want or expect.

Because the hairstylist is not valued so much as an artist or even a technician, but as a customer service representative, individual stylists become less important to the larger culture of the salon. In the excerpt below, for example, John discusses how a stylist, in some ways, is somewhat expendable as long as the culture of the salon is strong. He has obvious disregard for the individual once she or he leaves the salon:

I mean like Renee leaving. Fifty percent of her clientele came back. . . even when Renee left *initially*, some of her clients didn't follow her because they, the thing they were used to getting. And that's why it's important to us th-that I don't build our business on just . . . a stylist.

To John, customer loyalty is ensured, even when a stylist leaves, because a client has become accustomed to the atmosphere, the culture, the experience he or she receives at the salon. Also, for John, as indicated above, a high-performing stylist is one with access to that cultural affect, not necessarily the one with the highest technical skill: "Aaron is a perfect example of it. I'm not saying he's not a, a good hairstylist, but his customer service excels on everybody else's."

In this excerpt, John equates cultural affect to customer service. He does not really comment on his employee's technique or artistry as a stylist, but upon his customer service skills. Ultimately, then, all of the employees are viewed by John in relation to the salon and to his ultimate goal of profit.

> I'm the type of person you're gonna get along with because—but it's business. We can be friends, but respect this business. An' that's what I expect outta them . . . um, if you, if this is not where you wanna be, then find a place . . . um, I don' ask about people that used to work for us, because it's not . . . [*You don't ask about them? You mean how are they doing?*] Yeah, an' that's because that don' mean nothing to me.

John stresses that it is strictly a business relationship. Just as in the earlier excerpt, he talks about what he can "get out" of his employees. An employee who leaves has nothing to offer him in the way of profit, so he has no reason to continue a relationship with the person. This game-day approach to employee performance and development positions John as someone who has high expectations and the employee as being in constant try-outs.

Thus far we have examined some of the "what" of occupational practices as they relate to the goals, values, and constraints within the salon. By directing our gaze at the point of apprenticeship, our journey has provided us with a better view of the purposes and goals of work tasks as the participants of such activities view them, and the roles they take up in order to meet institutional goals.

As a place of practice, the salon provides us with:

- A robust site from which to examine the goal-oriented practices that constitute what it means to teach and to learn within that specific context
- A space from which to characterize the processes of how learning takes place, within the context of work, through the use of cultural tools that individuals designate to perform particular tasks
- A site where alternative points of view, culturally informed structures for participation, and meaning-making might be located and situated within the context of the African American community

Up to now, we have seen that what employers value as a tool or re-source may in fact be perceived differently by those who are expected to meet particular goals. In what follows, we will continue to examine such resources, focusing our attention on how effective the valued tools and resources are in meeting the goals of a community. In particular, we will focus on participants' views concerning the application of tools in order to accomplish goals and tasks and the origins of those tools.

TOOLS OF THE TRADE

Credentials, including college diplomas, are but one indicator of skill and a primary mechanism by which individuals signal to employers their potential to perform competently in a line of work (Orr, 1996). In Time Out hair sa-lon, located near Kuttin' Up, in a large midwestern city, being able to skill-fully perform tasks is not simply a matter of being licensed or credentialed. Rather, it is the ability to do something well that is dependent on and dis-played within interactions with others. One stylist's assistant characterizes the credentialing process as follows:

> School is broken into phases and it just give you the basics, how to put a roller in, the concepts of stuff. The first 12 weeks there's theory— theory is books, you do take some notes. It's all about the science of hair. You learn biology, anatomy of hair, the kinds of germs you might run into. Once you've covered the theory, you demonstrate, in phases, each skill on a mannequin and each has to be performed within a certain amount of time. Phase I is a combination of theory, where the teacher demonstrates on a mannequin each technique. Phase II is when you learn about chemical applications. You work on a man-nequin. With each mannequin you perform a different task. Phase III is color—learning how to apply color in different patterns, primary, tertiary, and secondary colors. The school supplies you with all of your tools—capes, irons, combs, luggage, etc. After each phase there is a 4-week clinic where you demonstrate, show what you've learned on someone's head and cultivate your people skills. (Stephanie)

Applying that which is acquired through credentialing also may involve a person's ability to respond to the unique demands of specific situations and contexts.[1]

> In [beauty school] my assistant has been introduced to the basics, the things that rain, sleet, or shine, I know I'm going to need in a given

day. She's been introduced to customer service, she knows how to interact with people, knowing how to serve people, how to maintain professionalism and serve it. It's kind of the idea that [clients] are here to escape, so you do whatever you have to. The curriculum in the salon is teaching them how to deal with what they won't expect, rather than the traditional curriculum, where it lays out what to expect. The thing you can expect is variance across customers. You're teaching [them] to expect the unexpected and how to apply what they know to each different thing. (Natasha)

It is important here to differentiate between the kinds of skills required for physical, manual tasks and the kinds of skills required in the *negotiation* of work tasks, which do not require physical labor and give the impression of effortless expertise, such as:

- Time management
- Picking things up quickly
- Being patient
- Being creative
- Being able to multitask

In addition to these skills are what one stylist's assistant calls "blind memory." Blind memory is the ability to instinctively and consistently "anticipate the needs of stylists" and to quickly execute problem solutions, thereby building strong rapport among staff members.

The most important tool you can have is memory. We ain't got no time to be writing stuff down. It's irritating I don't have time to be waiting for you. I've got four folks waiting. Keep your hands on things and develop an eye for what needs to be done without being told what it is you need to know to maintain the climate. It's like being blind. In the beginning I'm telling you exactly what to do, but very quickly, I do expect you to get it on your own. Everything you do helps the next thing you have to do. (Natasha)

This serves as an interesting contrast to the processes for learning in traditional classroom settings, where pen and paper serve as tools for documenting, organizing, and retrieving valued information.

When we were in hair school there's no point to take notes, your packets are your notes and it's up to you to apply what you know. Here you'd don't really have time to get your notebook and write stuff down, because by the time you do, there's something else that needs your time. It really depends, everybody has their own speed, maybe she'll catch on. (Stephanie)

Stephanie's view illuminates the possible schism between practice as work and school-based practices that involve documenting information, primarily for the purposes of assessment at a later date. Valued processes like note-taking and assessment, believed to aid learning and future application of skills, are not equally valued in this salon, where the process of learning is doing. Furthermore, while the general context of work attempts to reconcile this schism, rarely is it the other way around, where school-based practices attempt to account for "the next thing you have to do."

RIGGED SCRIPTS AS TOOLS OF THE TRADE

In the context of work, the principles for accomplishing goals (curriculum) can fail to account for the abstract details of task performance. Furthermore, in attempting to propel novice employees toward task completion through reliance on espoused (canonical) practice, employers often can "blind an organization's core to the actual and usually valuable practices of its members" (Brown & Duguid, 1991, p. 41). This includes noncanonical practices, such as social interaction. As others have argued regarding school and classroom settings, it is the actual practices of an institution that determine its success or failure (Dirkx, 1996; Hull & Schultz, 2002), where there is a close connection between literacy practices, identities, and discourses (Hamilton, 2006). Such practices may provide novice learners with a means for observing, understanding, and engendering the processes of problem solving that are inherent in accomplishing occupational tasks.

A sociocultural view of learning, as social construction, provides us with a useful lens through which to examine that framework both within the context of the hair salon and within classrooms. In this view, learners can be seen to construct their understanding through mediational means, out of a wide range of tools that include social and physical circumstances. Lave and Wenger's (1991) concept of "legitimate peripheral participation," for example, provides a lens through which to view learning as *becoming an insider to a community*. According to this concept, learners do not receive knowledge; rather they learn to function in a community by acquiring that community's subjective viewpoint and learning to speak its language (Brown & Duguid, 1991).

For example, in what follows, a novice/newcomer employee attempts to perform the front-end task of responding to a client's request over the phone.

Rahla: (on the phone) Anybody for shampoo? Well, we don't do style without shampoos, shampoo is part of it (pause) right . . . lemme see, hold on. (to Tanya) Do you know . . . these people want to come in for a style, for a wedding, they don't want shampoo, they just want style.

Tanya: They can't do that, wait a minute, is this the Shaneka Downes party? Did they say they wanted to see Dionne?

Rahla: Saturday at 9, she said she don't care who she see, she just want styles.

Ladiedra: OK see cuz I had one um (pause) somebody called and she's a bride and she wanted four of her bridesmaids to get their hair done . . .

Rahla: OK.

Ladiedra: . . . But they wanted Antonio to do it and they wanted to just get it styled and Antonio said that they don't do that here.

Rahla: Then we don't do that here, right, Terri?

Tanya: No. We don't do that.

Rahla: Right. (speaking into phone) Hello? Hi, you know what? I'd love to accommodate you but we only do shampoo with styles. (pause)

In the above exchange, Rahla, the novice, does not receive explicit, formal instruction on how to solve her problem of determining the correct line of action. Rather, what she receives is a set of behaviors and norms that characterize what others, in this case Tanya and Ladiedra, perceive as appropriate means for problem solution. Such resources become a part of that learner's repertoire of solutions—sets of beliefs (tools) that constitute an interpretive framework through which members of the culture make sense of phenomena (Lee, 1995). It is through such resources, in particular the narrative shared Ladiedra, that meanings and understandings are constructed. As a novice employee, Rahla unpacks institutional and systemic constructions of problem solving through a reconstructed narrative provided by Ladiedra. That narrative is not only a part of the interpretive process of meaning-making, it is also tied to the ways in which individuals in the salon critique human action. It is in this instance that Rahla, perhaps unintentionally, is being scaffolded into institutionally sanctioned norms for problem posing and problem solving. In doing so, she is discovering which resources to apply. Such resources become a part of that learner's repertoire of solutions.

Skilled practical thinking often seeks those modes of solution that are the most economical or that require the least effort—"We don't do that here." It involves the acquisition and use of specific knowledge that is functionally important to the larger activities in which problem solving is embedded. At the front end of Posh Salon, this is enacted in the context of the salon not as the intended curriculum (standard operating plan), but rather the improvised plan. Thus, Ladiedra doesn't issue a directive or the solution to the problem, but rather scaffolds the novice into the structure of problem posing and problem solving by presenting options to be considered, making transparent her repertoire of solutions by sharing a similar situation.

I want to argue that within the above example of accomplishing work tasks is a sharing of experiences that led to a collaborative, multi-voiced, dialogic problem solution. This solution operates in terms of shifting the problem terrain in order to solve the task at hand. This shifting is an aspect of "the goal-directed experience of working on the problem together" (Kuhn, 2015, p. 48). This goal-directed action benefits individuals' acquisition of new concepts "in the context of a [particular] problem requiring their application" (p. 48).

It is important, however, to acknowledge that in the world of work, people have few options for shifting problem terrain entirely—of redefining or reformulating problems. On many occasions, problems arise that have a general shape but not a definite formulation. One artful aspect of practical thinking, however, is to construct or redefine the problem that experience suggests will facilitate a solution. Skilled practical thinking is marked by flexibility—solving the "same problem" in different ways, each finely fitted to the occasion. Formal models of problem solving lead us to expect that repetitive problems will be solved by the same sequence of operations. However, such models may fail to account for the unexpected variability routinely displayed by expert team members.

On many occasions, problems arise that have a general shape but not a definite formulation. One artful aspect of practical thinking, however, is to construct or redefine the problem in a way that experience suggests will facilitate a solution. Skilled practical thinking is marked by flexibility— solving the "same problem" in different ways, each finely fitted to the occasion (Kuhn, 2012). As Stephanie suggests:

> The book gives you a guide for how to assess, but in practice you learn that you can't treat all people as if they was the same way the book says. (Stephanie)

From this perspective, learning in work means applying what you know in the moment, yet remaining flexible in anticipation of what's simultaneously

familiar and new. Such flexibility in meeting changing conditions *and* inge-
nuity in devising ways of meeting goals are aspects of improvisation, or
what I want to call rigging, within task performance. The process of rigging
involves the application of one's repertoire of solutions in both carrying out
the task and understanding the skilled processes required to do so. Inherent
in this process is the use of relevant cultural traditions and norms.

Within rigging, the particular skills for performing tasks act as scripts.
For example, blind memory. Recall Natasha's statement regarding practice:
"Keep your hands on things and develop an eye for what needs to be done
without being told what it is you need to know to maintain the climate. It's
like being blind."

The skillful act of "being blind"—using your hands and other affordances
—functions as a script for the novice. According to Gutierrez, Rymes, and
Larson (1995), such "scripts, as part of activity systems, incorporate stable
and predictable features; simultaneously scripts lend themselves to improvisation and it is this improvisational quality that accounts for the potential
for change and development" (p. 449). Furthermore, when viewed in light
of the institutional curriculum, rigged scripts can serve to counter the effects
of canonical teaching practices, which, as previously indicated, "blind an
organization's core to the actual and usually valuable practices of its members" (Brown & Duguid, 1991, p. 41).

In the hair salon, the cultural practice of creating and exchanging stories generates narrations of understanding. The social construction of these
narrations of understanding acts as repositories of accumulated wisdom,
or rigged scripts, that allow employees to circumvent the inadequacies of
standard operating plans. These rigged scripts are not only developed in
practice, but are preserved in community storytelling.

WHAT HAVE WE LEARNED?

Workplace learning is best understood in terms of repertoires of practice.
The central issue in learning is becoming a practitioner, not learning about
practice. This approach to development in the context of the salon draws attention away from abstract knowledge and cognitive processes, and situates
it in the hybrid space of community practices, in which knowledge takes on
significance.

In the Time Out and PA salons, participants appear to be more cog-
nizant, if not accepting, of the concept of rigging. Some demonstrate little
patience for the complexities of learning how to do it, a process that occurs
over time as it requires that novices "let go" and negotiate school-based
approaches and processes to learning with context-based approaches and

moment-to-moment realities. For example, when acknowledging her annoyance at one recent new hire's insistence on taking notes while working, Natasha states, "Why take notes? Who comes in early or stays up to study [their] notes anyway? Who's really studying when they go home after working all day? Not real-world folks!"

Yet we know that note-taking is a form of processing that supports retention for some, even if those notes are never read again. Natasha does not account here for the individual needs of learners, and disrespects this learner for her strategies, just as schools sometimes do.

Still, Natasha's view is an interesting one when contrasted to school-based-practices, of documenting what gets perceived as valuable "knowledge" for retention and use at a later date. This illuminates the possible schism between the expectations around learning set forth in schools and those practices maintained in work, where the process of learning consists of doing. Learning opportunities are viewed as occuring in the space of the individual's zone of proximal development (ZoPed), a concept that emphasizes the processes by which individual youth (as novices) are socialized into the practices of the dominant culture through their engagement with shared cultural norms, tools and experienced others within the group. The "informal" work that novices do to make sense of the formalized structure and institutional goals that frame practices is where learners either succeed or fail. Their ability to improvise successful strategies dictates how well they do. Likewise, for many students, learning in school is a "black box," where they don't understand the processes of how learning occurs nor is there a space within which to reflect on that learning (Lee, 2007). Arguably, successful learning in that context is contingent upon the degree of transparency of actual practice, between institutional curriculum and hidden curriculum, in homes and in schools. Practical thinking, thinking that is embedded in the larger purposive activities of daily life and that functions to achieve the goals of those activities, is illuminated in the context of work through descriptions of practice (Scribner, 1984).

Figure 3.1 illustrates the tensions that can exist within the salon as a context for teaching and learning (constituting formal and informal practices, which may overlap). As I've illustrated, such hybridity stimulates the transformation of work practice into a robust learning opportunity.

Sources for problem solving are simultaneously created and taken up in the spaces between experts and novices. These are critical hybrid spaces where participants make use of particular technologies, like language, in order to collaboratively construct knowledge, distribute and cope with task completion for success, and manage the everyday nuances of maneuvering within a culturally shared and situated site of labor (Majors, 2004, 2006). Additionally, I believe that the values, skills, and tools associated with the

Figure 3.1. Hybrid Activity as Rigged Script

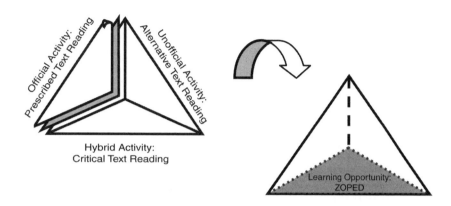

work that people do (e.g., being in the moment and ready for game day, having blind memory, attending an idea of the customer) are not bound to just one site, but have correspondence and implications across contexts, continuing to affect discourse practices and individual development.

IMPLICATIONS FOR SCHOOLING

Arguably, there is a gap in schools one between the institutional curriculum and the reality of students' lives. Investigations into salon practices indicate that similarly there is a gap between the institutional curriculum of work and the reality of the workers. Reconciliation of that gap is akin to a process of rigging. For example, Ladiedra, being intuitive about her work, applies scripts from her repertoire of solutions to assist the novice Rahla in carrying out the task and understanding/recognizing which skilled processes are required to do so. Inherent in this process is the use of relevant cultural traditions and norms, such as narrative. Such formats for problem solving can serve to scaffold novice employees into the community, while providing useful scripts for future problem-solving tasks.

As in many urban schools, where often the separation between home and school practices creates and sustains isolation between individuals within that context, there is a similar disconnect in the salon between the improvisational practices of workers and what is upheld as standard by the institution. The tools students come to school armed with to tackle academic tasks ultimately become of greater consequence than the tools schools introduce them to, as seldom are they taught how to apply those tools. The question is, like the novice learners in the salon, are children able to navigate the demands of school through the processes and tools with which they are familiar? Can they figure out what the hidden curriculum is? I imagine that the answer to these questions is yes, when they are given the opportunity and supports to do so.

Ultimately, the question is not can they and how, but rather what the impact of learning and development is over the life span and in work and school. As Rogoff (2003) contends, "development over the life span is inherently involved with historical developments of both the species and cultural communities, developments that occur in everyday moment-by-moment learning opportunities" (p. 51). Viewing "high test scores" as the most significant institutional goal and sole measure of learning outcomes, therefore, becomes problematic from this perspective, when student learning is viewed as becoming a participant of practice. In the context of schooling, particular processes for task completion are provided through formal instruction. However, they do not take into account the need for contextual modification and improvisation by learners.

CHAPTER 4

Cultural Border Crossing and the Narration of Social Texts

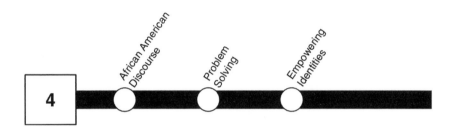

What are the intersections between participation in discourse communities, problem solving, and social and academic identities?

As mentioned earlier, people read social relations every day in daily life. In Chapter 3, for example, we learned that in PA salon the orientation of the task—understanding a client's aesthetic need—was determined, in part, by what the stylists deliberately read with regard to the "inside of a person to figure out what they really need on the outside." Such readings were influenced by external social and cultural values, as well as how those values aligned with the stylist's own.

I am reminded here of the teacher who reads her students and attempts to teach them based on her interpretations, which are shaped by local and distal factors. In other words, *what* the teacher views as the key task in accomplishing the instructional goal (e.g., identifying and understanding what is ironic about particular events within a stretch of text) intersects with her belief about how such tasks should be performed and the appropriate skills and tools for doing so.

In what follows, we return to Darlene and Ms. Addie as individually they narrate their readings of culture, class, and other social relations. We will examine how the other participants, in turn, read the women's narrations as a way of complex problem solving. Each woman manages this participation collaboratively with her social partners as she takes on important roles within the discourse, drawing from a toolkit of cultural resources to reason through events. This collaborative and coordinated reasoning is an aspect of social reading, where participants evaluate some action within events by protagonists (texts), whose actions, thoughts, and feelings are interpreted by the women in light of local notions of what is right, wrong, and just.

We will see how Ms. Addie and Darlene not only navigate across multiple discourses (border cross), but also construct and transmit their understandings of the world. The analysis of these narrations, through the lens of guided participation, closely examines each participant's (as a social actor) use of linguistic and cultural tools as instruments of (1) problem solving, (2) representing canonical relationships and values, and (3) interpreting and reading social texts. The questions we want to ask along the way are:

- How do people use cultural tools for readings of social texts?
- What role does identity play in individuals' problem posing and problem solving?
- How does the interaction between participants and the arrangement of their talk contribute to the meanings they create?

MS. ADDIE AND THE PROBLEM IN AMERICA

Ms. Addie was selected for this particular focus on skills in reading cross-cultural interactions because she was one of the most self-reflective and colorful participants in this study. Within Shoptalk, Ms. Addie narrates to her audience her experience during a cross-cultural encounter that takes place at a reading workshop meeting held at a local library. This narrated event is prompted by questions from those in the salon concerning Ms. Addie's costumed attire: as noted earlier, heavy, black military-style, lace-up boots, a sweeping floor-length, red and white chambray checkered skirt, long layered lace slip, white-breasted apron, long-sleeved white cotton shirt buttoned to the top with a rounded collar, and a white kerchief tied at the top to cover her hair. Undergirding this broader discussion, however, is Ms. Addie's earlier account of a cross-cultural encounter at the workshop meeting with a White female participant around the topic of teaching slavery in schools.

The socially constructed, narrative text presented here is situated within the broader interactional discussion of Ms. Addie's costumed attire and public reactions to it, in particular by her students and peers within the elementary school. This group discussion is prompted when Ms. Addie is asked about her day's events dressed as Harriet Tubman. This request brings the topic to the floor, which on the surface appears to be Ms. Addie's costume, but is also Ms. Addie's celebration of her ability to read the racialized subtext of the events and report on how she responds to them without buying into the assumptions of others.

> *Ms. Addie:* You know, I went to a workshop at the Newberry library on Saturday morning and they had all of these teachers. I mean this is a Saturday morning and people came and they turned some people away because the room was too small. But the one thing that they were trying to stress was we were coming together to develop concepts for how to teach about slavery.
>
> *From the audience:* Mmmm.
>
> *Ms. Addie:* And these folks, there was this one woman there who was White. And another one, a young Black woman. And they happened to be sitting on the same couch. One on one end, one on the other end. And so this guy said, "Is there anyone here who is having difficulty with this subject?" And so this one woman raised her hand and she said, "You know, I'm having difficulty because I teach the 6th grade, but I feel guilty, I, um, my family owned slaves."
>
> *From the audience:* Girrrlll. . . . Mmmm. (exaggerated eye rolling and eyebrow raising)
>
> *Ms. Addie:* And she said? "I have all of the books, I know how many people were sold, even their names. How much it cost. How much they paid for them."
>
> *Carmen:* She's got everybody in a book, huh?
>
> *Ms. Addie:* And everybody was looking at her. It's in her family.
>
> *From the audience:* Hmm.
>
> *Carmen:* In her family? I hear you.
>
> *Ms. Addie:* And she's like—she looks, she looks like she may be in her late 40s, if that old, and she said, "And I feel so guilty and I don't know what to do about it." And so then this other lady, the young lady, said—the other Black lady said, "Why?" She says "I feel guilty because," she says, "I feel uncomfortable because I, I've only been teaching 4 years, and I don't, I don't want to teach the kids in a way where the kids will become angry? I want to teach it so that it's—it's objective, they will learn from it." And, uh, so these two—but after these two people said what they said—'cuz you could see the tension in the air. There was all kind of people, Black people, Hispanic people, and Jewish people—uh, but it was a kinda in the air, it was tension. But after these two people said what they said, it just cleared the air. It was an awesome class and I am so glad I went because this is a problem in America. Teachers who say they feel uncomfortable teaching about slavery.

The Social Reader

Ms. Addie's narration illuminates some important things with regard to the appropriation of cultural tools through the skill of social reading. When we view the above narrative event through the lens of guided participation, what stands out in the analysis is the interconnectedness of language and social power at the levels of production and enactment. This socially constructed reading of the events presented by Ms. Addie invites an awareness of the social process and structures by which participants create meaning and illustrates how people positioned on the borders between cultural groups/discourse communities may use cultural tools for reading social relations.

The world as socially constructed, narrative text is part and parcel of how people make sense of the world. The skills required to read social text share important qualities with what some call literary schemata (Graves & Frederiksen, 1996; Lee, 1992; Van Den Broek, 1994). In culturally and politically constructed contexts—like beauty salons, barbershops, and classrooms—people read, write, talk, and think about real ideas and information in order to ponder and extend what they know, communicate with others, present their points of view, understand, and be understood (Langer, 1987). This sense-making process bridges action and consciousness in culturally and linguistically appropriate ways that involve skills that are important to domain-specific teaching and learning (e.g., secondary language arts). Reading within cultural and linguistic contexts involves an active evaluation of actions by protagonists, whose actions, thoughts, and feelings are interpreted in light of local notions of what is right and wrong, just and unjust.

Such reading is a literacy skill that adult and adolescent cultural border crossers rehearse and develop through their participation within specific, socially contingent discourses and/or through their movement across different kinds of discourse communities. It is in the activity of having one's hair done that participants, like Ms. Addie, take up an opportunity to read social relations, both through their own positionings within the Shoptalk discourse and through their shared experiences of being positioned in particular ways within society.

Beginning in the first line, Ms. Addie positions herself as a cultural border crosser of two discourse communities, one within the book club discussion and one within the salon. In doing so, she makes a distinction between her participation and positioning in the two communities by characterizing the participants of the workshop as "these folks," despite the fact that she is a participant as well. This positioning, established through rhetorical structures, places Ms. Addie in the role of social reader of race and gender, in which she revoices what can be considered the official point of view of the Newberry (institutional) discourse community.

Ms. Addie accomplishes this by setting up the characters of the event, stressing racial distinctions, "one woman," changing volume and intonation when adding the qualifier, "who was White." When Ms. Addie says, "Black woman," her intonation rises sharply, in contrast to when she said, "White woman." This contributes to the establishment of an ironic tension for the listeners to pick up on, as in this event Ms. Addie doesn't set up the reported speech of the White woman differently at the outset, but slows down for emphasis when she gets to the crucial point, which is: "her family owned slaves." These responses are spaced out, giving time for dramatic ironic effect.

Interdisciplinary research on African American discourse, verbal genres, and interactions has been voluminous and has provided insights into the social construction of languages and the complexity of speech events (Bakhtin, 1981; Goffman, 1974; Gumperz, 1982; Ochs, 1990). Ms. Addie's reading of the event is structured by an African American narrative style in which she directs the speech encounter, with the audience participating minimally. For example, in the illustration above, participants are cooperating with respect to the dramatic tension. The jointly shared responses of the audience members—both spontaneous, exaggerated eye gestures and verbal responses—indicate their engagement and signal the gravity of the narrative's turn and their mutual understanding as to the motives of Ms. Addie's linguistic act. The narrative sequencing in this context of Shoptalk, therefore, is produced jointly by an active audience, who by virtue of their participation bring a shared knowledge of both Shoptalk as a genre of conversational discourse and the norms of AAE to bear on its constructions. Each participant contributes to the representations of Shoptalk and narrative structure of the activity. They do this first by agreeing on the definition of the situation (Wertsch, 1985), which is Shoptalk, and second by implementing a system of semiotic mediation, that is, "black modes of discourse" (Smitherman, 2000, p. 103) as a sign of agreement. Ms. Addie's positioning within the discourse is important, as it illuminates a critical issue in the development of this theory of reading the Other. The paralinguistic features conveyed in actions, motions, and gestures of the participants make visible the links and dimensions of a broader and otherwise external African American community. For example, Ms. Addie itemizes the White woman's claims with parallel intonational contour, giving laundry-list cohesion, creating an easy listening pattern, and holding listener interest. Here, Ms. Addie reports more speech of the White woman, giving her speech a soft, emotional tone marked by lower volume, a breathier quality, and rising intonation toward the end of the phrase with a phase-final drop in intonation. This implies perhaps another kind of dramatic tension, one that is ironic, but unstated, in which the audience as readers of this narrative must infer its significance within the text as well as the author's (Ms. Addie's) intentions. While reading this racialized subtext, Ms. Addie appears to also be reading the responses of her audience and acknowledges their positionings through that reading.

Because Ms. Addie knows that the White woman's openness in the story led to a positive outcome, she may be portraying the White woman in a positive light to counter the wary and negative responses the tale has elicited from her audience within the salon. Note that it is here that the notion of a critical reading of events in text is illuminated, as participants' prior understandings of the phenomenon (White enactment of power) and resistance to that phenomenon (wary responses) take center stage and get taken up. If this is the case, Ms. Addie may want her audience to be receptive, so she is sensitive to their stance and adjusts hers to get the most empathetic outcome. This is a skill, developed and displayed by border crossers, involving both reading and representation—both receptive and productive aspects.

Like Ms. Addie, all people are at times put in the position of taking up contradictory identities or points of view. But her narrative is one told by someone who is continually "on the borders" in her social positions vis-à-vis dominant society and/or who has less power. Such people, those who lack power in dominant society, often may find themselves experiencing tension and discord. Theirs is a point of view that gets read within and across power structures, just as Ms. Addie reads the points of view across the two contexts. And they must read how others read them (and others) as a matter of survival. Power is about relations of difference, and particularly about the effects of differences in social structures. The constant unity of language and other social matters ensures that language is entwined in social power in a number of ways; language indexes power, expresses power, is involved regardless of whether there is contention over and a challenge to power. Power does not derive from language, but language can be used to challenge power, to subvert it, to alter distributions of power in the short and long term (Wodak & Meyer, 2001).

Social Reading of Narrative Texts as a Kind of Problem Solving

Reading from "points of view" is what makes social reading a particularly useful skill. It is also what undergirds the problem-solving potential embedded within such readings. In the above narrative, Ms. Addie revoices an institutional point of view, that the problem in America is "teachers who say that they feel uncomfortable teaching about slavery." She presents her skilled use of the social reading of an institutional position on slavery and its teaching. This is the presentation of a "problem" situation in that it appears, at least for the institutional voices, that this is a given and should be taken at face value. However, as indicated here, those within the salon react to this point of view, a reaction in line with Ms Addie's emotional stance: that someone feeling uncomfortable with talking about slavery is subject to question. In revoicing this institutional (official) point of view, Ms. Addie characterizes the "problem" as an expressed discomfort with the teaching of slavery.

Ms. Addie's opposition and that of the other women suggest that this problem should not be taken at face value. This opens up the door for "intellectual work," which consists of a series of rhetorical questions of the audience, a preacher-like rhetorical strategy. Ms. Addie knows she has developed her case to a sympathetic audience, and she ups the emotive ante, making room for a redefinition of the "problem" through subsequent readings. In this sense, Ms. Addie's narrative serves as a cultural and psychological tool for telling not only what has happened, but also why it happened (Bruner, 1990).

In what follows, Ms. Addie unpacks the official problem through a series of sequenced steps, slowly and predictably, garnering audience support and sympathy, making for a sound platform on which to redefine or reread the initial problem through artful deconstruction and reconstruction.

> *Ms. Addie:* But see this is the whole point is ownership. If you know that your folks are responsible for this, and all these?—Do you know how many years have passed? People have not done anything? That's over a hundred years?
> *Wendi:* What do you mean people haven't done anything?
> *Ms. Addie:* I'm talking about people who know that . . .
> *Carmen:* Reparations?
> *Ms. Addie:* Slavery has occurred.
> *Audience:* Mm-hmm.
> *Ms. Addie:* There have been, um, people have been killed. Lynched. Jim Crow laws. Intentional, um, rules set aside so that Black people are affected adversely. And—and nobody—your mother, your grandmother, your uncles, aunts, all your family, all these people in this whole country? They didn't do anything about it!
> *Wendi:* What can they do?
> *Ms. Addie:* I mean, what's everybody they're in denial. A lot of them figure, "It wasn't me." A lot of 'em say, "It wasn't me. It was somebody before me." It was my great-great-grandmother." Whatever. You see, that does not relieve you.
> *Wendi:* I agree with you.

Ms. Addie's experience and identity as an African American community member—and as a veteran classroom teacher—enables the application of a socially preferred mode of problem solving within this context. In the above excerpt, Ms. Addie aptly decomposes the official problem, which is to say that the problem is not discomfort, but rather guilt, by introducing an alternative (unofficial) text to the procedure. Here, Ms. Addie gets to the heart of her argument, following more statements of agreement from the other speakers. In introducing an alternative point of view, Ms. Addie redefines the initial problem, hence shifting the problem space through rhetorical and discursive strategies, rooted in the African American narrative tradition.

It is through narrative that Ms. Addie creates meaning for herself and her position as a member of cultural minority group. She unpacks institutional and systemic constructions of identity through a reconstructed narrative. In effect, narrative is not only part of the interpretive process of meaning-making, but is also tied to the ways in which Ms. Addie critiques human action. Ms. Addie uses narrative to take an ethical stance on those who are uncomfortable with teaching slavery, and in her deconstruction, she repositions this sense of discomfort as guilt. This narrative understanding is filtered through her own autobiography and her positioning as an African American female. Accordingly, narrative is part of the process of how Ms. Addie and the other women come to see themselves and their own shared life history. In other words, the self is narratively constructed (Grimes, 1975). Furthermore, narrative is the lens through which these cultural border crossers make meaningful their experiences (as individuals) and the experiences of others in the context of the salon, namely, by understanding themselves and their positions relationally. Thus, narrative provides ethical dimensions to experience, and as a ritualized practice it is inherently tied to the creation of value systems (Grimes, 1975).

For example, Ms. Addie seems to really stress the term *ownership*, by practically sounding out each syllable. This is done through rhetorical questions of the audience, following the AAE discursive tradition of call and response, a preacher-like, rhetorical strategy. The last few phrases of her statement are marked by rising intonation at the end, each sentence ending higher than the preceding one. She continues in AAE rhetorical style and strategy with parallel structures between *killed* and *lynched,* and a second, slightly different set with *laws,* and *Crow laws.*

When enumerating a long list of kin, she makes dramatic delay of the main point that nothing so far has been done. She sets this argument up slowly and predictably, garnering audience support and sympathy. This makes for a sound platform on which to pontificate and take a moral stance. Ms. Addie also begins to evoke an "us" versus "them" ideal with her pronoun usage, something she began at the beginning of the presentation of the narrative event. This us versus them positioning is heightened as Ms. Addie constructs multiple roles (revoicing) within the narrative, playing both her part in the story as well as that of the White people whom she encounters. She constructs these identities as distinct in her speech by use of prosodic variance along the lines of rate of speech, volume, inflection (partly intonational contour), as well as characterization. In the following sequence, Ms. Addie continues to make the case for why the problem must be redefined in light of other considerations.

"I WASN'T SCARED OF THEM, THEY WERE SCARED OF ME!"

Analysis of Ms. Addie's salon conversation needs to consider both receptive and productive aspects of narration of her cross-cultural encounters—both her reading and oral production of social texts. It is important to note that in the context of the salon, Shoptalk is both situationally and culturally specific. It refers to the talk that is engaged in many African American beauty salons (and arguably barbershops) between regular participants, employing shared discourse norms with a well-established cultural and historical base.

In what follows, Darlene describes to a group of listeners her own cross-cultural encounter at a resort in the remote mountains of Arizona. Undergirding this narrative is an account of what took place at a local bar near the resort, in which Darlene encountered a White male patron. In the hair salon, this narrative is situated within an informal discussion of interstate travel within the United States and the problems that can occur, particularly when that travel occurs in sites not frequently visited by African Americans. This group discussion was prompted when Darlene, the animator, was queried about her recent travels by Ms. L., a client. Her request brought the topic—which on the surface appeared to be interstate travel—to the floor, but the general message was Darlene's celebration of her ability to read the racialized subtext of the event and report on how she responded to it without buying into the assumptions of the White patron in the bar:

> *Darlene:* But the interesting part was this man at the bar comes up to
> me and he goes, um, it was like our—almost the last day that we
> was there. He goes "Uh, you know there's something very fascinat-
> ing about you." And I say, "Fascinating about me, what could be
> fascinating about me?" He goes, "Just the way that you walked
> into here, and, um, being the only Black girl, and you know we
> don't get Black people." And I say, "Is that a fact?"
> *Audience:* (loud laughter and foot stomping)

Darlene: He goes, "But, the only Black person in here and the way you just came in here and started shootin' pool and actin' like it was no problem." He said, "Don't you have just a slight bit of fear?" I go, "No, I don't."

Audience: (laughter)

Darlene: Um, he goes, "You didn't?" He said, "You had no fear at all?" I said, "Not at all." He goes, "Not the slightest little bit?" I said, "No!" I said, "I believe in predestination. And so, if I were to get killed up here I wouldn't be concerned about it because that was my destination."

Audience: (laughter)

Darlene: ". . . You, you know what I'm saying? And so therefore, you know when I walked in here, I didn't even think about what you may or may not do to me. That was not even a thought in my mind. That's because, see that's something that you would have to live with. And I think, uh, see my ultimate goal is to meet my maker anyway. So are you trying to tell me that you would deliver me there?" He goes, "Oh no, no, no." I said, "Oh, well I was, you know, just spouting out the same kind of concerns you were having."

Audience: (loud laughter, foot stomping) Uh-huh.

Darlene: And from that point on, it was like whatever Johnny and I wanted, it was there, right there.

Audience: Uh-huh, uh-huh.

Darlene: And the last day that we were there he was so amazing. It was like everybody in the bar just came in to say goodbye, and we would go down and shoot pool and so we'd come in to say goodbye. That man gave me the biggest hug.

Audience: Is that right?

Darlene: Girl, I done had so many hugs I thought my little back was gone break.

Audience: (laughter, foot stomping)

Darlene: They were scared. They were, they were scared of me.

Audience: Yeah, yeah.

 Darlene: I wasn't scared of them.

Audience: Yeah, yeah. Yeah.

Darlene: They were scared, of me.

Narrative Sequencing and Dialogicality

Three key observations can be made with regard to Darlene's rendering of her cross-cultural experience. The first is that the narrative structure above contributes to a dialogic group dynamic, which in itself contributes to self-affirmation and the presentation of a contested identity. Beginning in Line 1, Darlene's participant event is structured by an AAE narrative style in which she directs the speech encounter, with the audience participating minimally. For example, beginning with line 8, "(loud laughter and foot stomping)," to lines 19, 29, and 33, "(laughter)," and ending at line 40, ratified participants employ call and response throughout the narrative. This feature of AAE is "the spontaneous verbal and nonverbal interaction between speaker and listener in which all of the speaker's statements ('calls') are punctuated by expressions ('responses') from the listener" (Smitherman, 2000, p. 104). Such paralinguistic features, conveyed in actions, motions, and gestures such as foot stomping, and tone and pitch such as the uproar of laughter, make visible the links and dimensions of a broader and otherwise external African American speech community.

Although the experience of going to Arizona was not shared, within Shoptalk the narrative was collaboratively produced and functioned as a presentation of localized community kinship. Contributing to the narrative structure of the above illustration are AAE norms for talk. For example, the increase in frequency of audience response in lines 8 through 11 indicates a change in mood and narrative structure. Darlene maintains her role as narrator by keeping pitch contours constant, while the audience boosts the energy, which indicates the scene has been set and the action can now begin. Here, Darlene and the other participants co-construct the progression of the narrative.

Among the women in the hair salon, dialogic harmony is achieved and viewed throughout the rendering of the narrative through the responses of the audience (lines 8, 12, 17, 26, 29, and 35) to Darlene's calls. Such responses serve to signal the ends and beginnings of each part of the story. Within the structure of this culturally shared and situated discourse there is more than one narrator, as each member provides a support to the other in sensemaking. This speaks to the participation framework of talk in the salon as it brings the shared understanding and acceptance of a culturally rooted past—for example, the use of AAE norms—into the present, making visible specific structures for reasoning that move across boundaries of setting, space, and time. These linguistic and paralinguistic features of AAE establish rapport among speakers and serve as a transformative lens through which to perceive, make sense of, and challenge an external and competing point of view. This brings us to a second point, which is the use of narrative structure within the salon to contest an imposed identity.

Darlene's individual voice within the localized and collective context of Shoptalk establishes a cultural and linguistic connection among the participants. This connected voice affirms the humanity, specialness, and right to

exist and define oneself (Hill-Collins, 2000) that the women share against
the backdrop of the invisibility inherent in the objectification Darlene faces
in her encounter with the White man. Darlene displays her skills at Shoptalk before a collective audience that possesses the cultural skills to engage.
Like the hair salon, the local bar also can be viewed as a discursive context
in which ways of being are characterized by notions of race, gender, class,
and talk. However, in the instance where culturally significant verbal genres
(such as verbal inventiveness, signifying, and reading a person) are introduced within the noninclusive oppositional contexts of the bar, they can
serve to erode and disrupt particular images and positionalities.

In lines 3 through 6, for example, Darlene's identity and stance within
the bar are characterized by an onlooker as "fascinating." Her response
in line 4, however, "what could be fascinating about me?" sets up a reply
from the onlooker, who makes visible what is already obvious to Darlene,
that she is the only Black person in the bar and that her presence is a rar-
ity. Rather than announce publicly to her onlooker that this comes as no
surprise to her, Darlene chooses to appear surprised, an act on her part that
is unknown to her onlooker but obvious to her audience in the salon. Here,
the response of the audience acts as an indicator not only of engagement,
but of mutual understanding regarding the motive surrounding Darlene's
act—to appear ignorant of a very obvious fact in the presence of the White
man she has encountered. This verbal inventiveness, used here as a ploy, is
well understood and documented within the African American community
during cross-racial encounters and is exemplified within African American
literature (Lee, 1993).

Furthermore, based on the jointly shared response of the audience,
such inventiveness is perhaps expected and reflects a rapport and shared
point of view. What is more, is that for each participant, the world outside
the salon can be perceived not just through the eyes and ears of the local, but through the shared understanding of signifying, a Black mode of
social discourse generally invoked to make a point through an exchange
of boasts or insults. Here the presentation of signifying, employed by Darlene in her encounter, makes visible to us a culturally shared landscape,
removed from the present but generated in the salon through community
culture and style.

Both Darlene and Ms. Addie narrate and read social texts in situations
of cultural contact, and each constructs her own counternarrative texts in
response to these readings. Each reads subtle social cues, interprets those
cues based on her own sets of experiences in the world, and then presents
her interpretation in a way that is shaped by her reading of her audience,
and of her audience's reading of her. These skills are literacy skills, ones that
are bidialectical in nature, and serve as both cultural and cognitive resources

for participants. They are literacy skills in that they reveal the subject's attention to fine details for:

1. conveying nuances of meaning, including in wording, tone, stance, and subject positioning;
2. the reader's capacity to engage with both the "official," or surface, text and its subtexts;
3. recognition of and accommodation to different points of view; and
4. the construction of new texts that are appropriately worded and shaped for particular audiences. This includes audiences with shared assumptions, as well as those that are multiple and contradictory.

It is important not to confuse the form of reading discussed here with the kinds of reading that rely on the knowledge and understanding of particular graphic symbol systems. However, the reading of culture, class, and social relations, and the expression of counter-texts in response to those readings, are important skills for higher levels of engagement with written texts. These skills, which are rehearsed and developed through engagement in social encounters that cross lines of race, ethnicity, culture, class, and power, are in fact potentially powerful skills for the reading of all kinds of texts. They are tools that can be used to disrupt and erode borders of culture, gender, race/ethnicity, and social class in that students become empowered to talk back to disempowering texts.

As African American women in a White-dominant society, each participant develops these skills through interactions with those who have more formal or institutionalized social power than she. These interactions provoke dissonance, and it is in the resolution of that dissonance that participants cultivate the ability to read different points of view. Students who do not experience such dissonance—those whose own point of view neatly aligns with the dominant perspectives they encounter in school texts—are less likely to cultivate the capacity to recognize different perspectives, or to challenge them. I am reminded here of the point that Harding (1987) makes in her explication of feminist standpoint theory—that those with less privilege are often able to see social class relations more clearly than those with more privilege because it is in the interest of the latter not to see their own privilege. Although all people may find themselves in positions in which they feel compelled to take up contradictory identities, perspectives, and points of view, for members of groups that historically have been denied social power, the recognition and cultivation of alternative points of view—and the understanding of when and where to display such readings, and when and where to keep them subterfuged—may be important for survival. Research on the linguistic and cultural practices of non-"mainstream" groups often has focused on performances and practices of literacy: how people talk and how they write. It is also important, as in the above salon discourse, to contend with the receptive dimensions of engagement in literate practice: how people observe, listen, read, and take up social texts. Such readings shape acts of authorship: the close link between reading and writing, both the word and the world.

The literary philosopher Mikhail Bakhtin (1986) considered readers to be authors and the act of reading to be a dialogue between a text already produced and a reactive text created by a reader. Such a perspective transforms the traditional concept of reading into a contingent dialogic process, in which the reader becomes a border crosser in the process of reading. As applied to narratives of cross-cultural experience as text, social actors can be viewed not only as readers of narrated life texts, but also as authors of emergent narrative texts. In other words, narrator and audience are not fixed roles, but situated roles in which culturally shared norms and tools mediate who the reader is and who or what gets read.

Participants' roles are constituted not only by the creative and idiosyncratic intentions of individuals, but also through the historical traditions of discourses. Such historical traditions are culturally situated and include the literate ability to read context and the functional knowledge and use of "contextualization cues" (Gumperz, 1999). Such readings are part of the discourse, in which social positions (or perspectives) are "created from which people are invited, summoned to speak, act, read and write, think, feel, believe and value in certain characteristic, historically recognizable ways, in combination with their own individual style and creativity" (Gee et al., 1996, p. 10).

Social Reading of Narrative Texts as Empowering Identities

This process of social reading, making sense of the world through Shoptalk, is transformative. Verbal genres, norms for talk, and the style of presentation "alter the entire flow and structure of mental functions" (Wertsch, del Rio, & Alvarez, 1995, p. 23). This is clearly the case for AAE use within Shoptalk. Social reading accomplishes this by determining the structure of a new instrumental act, just as a technical tool "alters the process of a natural adaptation by determining the form of labor operations" (Wertsch, 1985, p. 93). In other words, for the individual participant, AAE changes how the problem, issue, or goal will be presented or solved. This leads to the third and final point: how Darlene's reading of cross-cultural texts through narrative is an empowering event.

For example, in lines 14 through 18, Darlene's insistence that she is not fearful of being "the only Black person" in the bar challenges the assumptions of the White onlooker. This places her in a position of power, in that she has the ability to alter those assumptions through her single response. Such repositioning of power disrupts and erodes the man's binary thinking (White/Black, woman/man, frightened/confident) and the controlling image of a passive, frightened, defenseless outsider. Darlene replaces this imposed, objectified status with one of spiritual subjectivity, humanization, and confidence. Furthermore, in Darlene's utterances, "That's because, see that's something that you would have to live with. And I think, uh, see my ultimate goal is to meet my maker anyway. So are you trying to tell me that you would deliver me there?" Darlene aligns herself oppositionally to the White man by voicing and strong emphasis, "not me." This communicative task highlights the conflict between Darlene's and the White man's sociocultural assumptions and draws attention to the emergence of what I have referred to elsewhere as Hair Say (Majors, 2004)—the dyadic/dependent relationship within speech events between public gendered and racialized speech, gendered roles within the broader cultural community, cultural definitions of such roles, the evaluation of presentation of style, and the AAE norms and meanings that thread them together.

These gendered and racialized attributes contribute to how participants make meaning of and within the multiple environments they navigate on a day-to-day basis. They also contribute to individuals' interpersonal decisionmaking processes, social representations within and across groups, self-perceptions, and understandings of the ways in which the world takes them into account as racial beings. For example, it is clear that Darlene views herself as a "spiritual individual" (i.e., human being)—she was just being herself regardless of her race and others'—while the White man used a racialized lens to evaluate the appropriateness of Darlene's presence and behavior. In other words, the man views Darlene as a racialized individual (a Black woman). Thus, there exists a conflict/problem between the two conceptualizations of Darlene's identity, which is negotiated and resolved securely within the context of the salon.

Beginning with line 11, in which the point of the story is relayed in a highly performative fashion, Darlene constructs multiple voices within the narrative, playing both her part in the story and that of the White man with whom she interacted in Arizona. She constructs these two identities as distinct in her speech by use of prosodic variance—rate of speech, volume, and inflection (partially intonational contour)—as well as characterization. Darlene "speaks" in the voice of the man first by lowering the volume of her speech as well as departing from the intonational pattern she set up earlier, namely, a rising intonation toward the end followed by a drop at the very end of utterances. She also depicts herself as "cool" to the man's "fool" by marking the reporting of her own speech with flatter intonational contour and quick responses. She reports her speech as if she answered each of the man's inquiries quickly and calmly without deliberation. She also reports the man as having stressed her actions (walking a certain way) and status as a Black woman as the focal points of his speech, which may or may not have been the case during the actual encounter, but are important to Darlene's delivery and so are constructed is needed. This emphasizes what Darlene finds salient about the encounter, further contextualizing her character by the man's words, without her needing to return to the narrator mode to continue setting the scene.

The content of Darlene's message, combined with the form of her delivery, is illustrative of an expressive, self-affirming text, which serves to challenge and contest the externally defined, controlling images used to justify Black women's objectification as the Other (Hill-Collins, 2000). This is illustrated in line 6, a pivotal exchange in which Darlene reads dialect on the man with, "Is that a fact?" As a verbal genre, "reading occurs whenever a speaker denigrates another to his or her face in an unsubtle and unambiguous manner" (Morgan, 1998, p. 262). The African American notion of reading as an interpretive practice also occurs through the process of reading dialect, when members of the African American community contrast or otherwise highlight obvious features of AAE in an unambiguous manner to make a point (Morgan, 1998). This is the first time Darlene reports her speech as having overt AAE features in contrast to the man's "non-AAE-ness" and the previously unmarked status of her prior speech. The phrase has the intonation, stress, and voice quality that often are associated with the hand-on-hip, neck-back-and-forth, eye-contact stance common to signifying. However, Darlene does not lose her cool; she simply contrasts her demeanor with his (and somewhat with her own prior speech) by this performative prosodic shift. The salon audience picks up on this marking and responds actively. Darlene participates in the laughter, marked by the voice quality at the beginning of line 9, and shifts back into her reported speech of the man. Here, she attributes repetitive phrase structure to the man's speech, to preserve the continuity and cohesiveness of the narrative. While the man engages in this structural repetition, marked by question-like rises of intonation at the end of each phrase, Darlene responds by breaking the pattern he set in terms of stress/rhythm, volume, and voice quality. She responds with a quick deadpan, "No, I don't." With flat intonational contour, and coolness, Darlene presents herself as refusing to reify the pattern established by the man in his questioning.

The man is reflected in much the same way by Darlene's speech reporting for the rest of the selection. She responds to his repeated questioning with a philosophical explanation in which she takes on the role of direct leader of the discussion. Both in her narration and the report of her own speech, she stresses the pronoun *I* continually. So, along with prosodic contrast to the man, and the depiction of a self-assured and cool Darlene, she further focuses the narrative on her own competence by aligning the speech with a self-direction and focus (via indexical pronoun use). She signifies a bit further (in a nondirect way at first) by making a jump from his questions about her concern with safety to a specific concern with murder. She says, without trepidation, what he might have been thinking and then dismisses the whole thing. As Darlene expounds on the reason for her lack of fear, the volume and stress of her speech increase. Certain words are punched home, compounded with even more stressed usage of *I* and *me*. This aggressive and forward speech emasculates the man's position without her attacking or even directly accusing him of anything. In effect, she makes an indirect joke of his naivete while ensuring her own empowered stance.

Darlene positions the question at the end of her philosophizing in such a way as to take him off guard and show that she does not assume he is trustworthy even though she admitted no fear. He responds in a predictably emasculated way, and Darlene latches onto his response with an indirect comment, which undermines the integrity of his entire line of questioning. At this point, the audience again responds to her verbal prowess, and she ties up the exchange with a claim to victory. Finally, in line 21, Darlene steps away from the report, laughing and asking the audience, "You know what I'm saying?" By this she momentarily steps out of the heated exchange to check in with her audience and reaffirm her buoyancy in the situation. The audience can assume that Darlene has a clear goal of making a claim as a participant who embodies these roles in both the hair salon and the bar. Darlene presents her claim in the final lines, when she declares that it was the patrons of the bar who were afraid, and not she, as their resistant actions transformed to displays of affection. We can assume that the actions and understandings of the individuals in the bar (and the audience in the salon) transform through the mediational power of language. Not only does language serve to connect the individual, the community, and the activity; it is an agent of transformation, acting as a means of influencing and thus transforming others inside and outside the group.

In choosing to tell her personal experience, Darlene must have formed her own predetermined points to convey, although other meanings would emerge through the conversational process. In other words, she is at least clear about what to narrate and why she wants to say something about the narrated event. Her selection of a certain "story" to tell is meaningful to her, but the lesson or the instructional meanings she wants to convey are left unsaid and invite the audience's interpretation. The restatement of her story, "I wasn't scared of them, they were scared of me," summarized the narrative without making explicit the point of who is supposed to be scared of whom and why one should be afraid of the other. Rather, such restatement directs the audience's thinking to interpret the unstated instructional meanings of the narrated event centering on the issue of racial conflict.

WHAT HAVE WE LEARNED?

In the above illustrations of Shoptalk, both Darlene and Ms. Addie relate their own experiences of being in contact zones. Each woman's narrative is represented to an audience that shares a core set of experiences and linguistic norms. Like that of Ms. Addie, Darlene's positioning within the discourse, in the process of representing her reading of the cross-cultural encounter, was among people with whom she felt comfortable and familiar. This group dynamic becomes evident within the analysis when we view the linguistic norms and cultural border crossing through the lens of guided participation.

Although hundreds of miles apart, in the contexts of both Darlene's and Ms. Addie's salons, the use of AAE norms in narrative production serves to minimize the distance between the participants. Such minimization, from a sociocultural perspective, is very important. First, it highlights how the collective activity of participants, as well as the kinds of interpersonal engagements and arrangements available to them, is both context-specific, yet moves across space and time by way of meditational tools, such as language. Additionally, participation in this socially and culturally mediated production "requires engagement in some aspect of the meaning of the shared endeavor, but not necessarily in symmetrical or even joint action. A person who is actively observing and following the decisions made by another is participating, whether or not he or she contributes directly to the decisions as they are made" (Rogoff, 1995, p. 147). For example, Ms. Addie is reflecting on border-crossing incidents, but she is recounting her experiences to an audience of insiders. The language that she uses to recount this episode reflects this.

Among the often-told stories within the salon while Darlene was present were those of the African American participants' cross-cultural interactions with White Americans. What I found interesting about Darlene's narrative, in relation to cultural border crossing, was how the structure of the narratives she shared contributed to a dialogic group dynamic within the salon. Narratives produced within Shoptalk provide a foundation from which to view the dialogic quality of voice in the hair salon. Dialogicality, according to Bakhtin (1986), precedes both utterance and voice. The utterance is filled with dialogic overtones that include the dialogic orientation between the utterances of one person and the utterances of another. Hence, in Shoptalk, dialogic harmony is achieved and viewed throughout the rendering of the entire narrative through the responses of the audience to the speaker.

Additionally, within the collective context of Black women's communities, the expression of individual voice is important for self-affirmation (Hill-Collins, 2000). According to Hill-Collins, "One can write before a nameless, faceless audience, but the act of using one's voice requires a listener and thus establishes a connection. For African American women the listener most able to pierce the invisibility created by Black women's objectification is another Black woman" (p. 104).

Such a group dynamic and narrative structure provide insight into participants' readings of the social and cross-cultural relations that may not have been apparent in the actual encounter. I also found it interesting how both Darlene and Ms. Addie report on their roles within the encounters, how each positions herself in relation to the other participants by enacting multiple voices and identities rather than those imposed upon her, and how each dismantles the power relations implicit in the context of the encounter while simultaneously constructing her own powerful identity.

Finally, both Darlene and Ms. Addie are moving across borders and acting in two social situations, neither of which includes members of the other group. Yet, as we've seen, each social actor reports in a social situation (Shoptalk) that does not include members of both groups (Black and White) and around a topic (U.S. slavery) directly related to ancestors of both groups. How each woman positions herself in relation to the other participants across contexts is key, therefore, and the positioning is carried out by these social actors by enacting multiple voices and identities, rather than taking up those imposed upon them. Additionally, how each dismantles the power relations implicit in the context of her encounter, while simultaneously constructing her own powerful identity, is also considered. It is in the narration of each woman's experience that we can gain insights into their readings of social relations. It is also within these narrations that we may view the problem-solving potential embedded within such readings.

IMPLICATIONS FOR SCHOOLING

Narratives produced and interpreted within Shoptalk provide a lens by which to view participants' reality, as well as their readings of social relations. As the above analysis indicates, active participants of Shoptalk, like many of our students, encounter social, cultural, and linguistic borders. Unlike in many classrooms, however, participants of Shoptalk collectively and publicly cross those linguistic borders through linguistic norms embedded within AAE for the purposes of making sense of the world. The embedded nature of such linguistic norms is important to note, as it makes certain linguistic borders less visible to the outside reader of these social events. For the participants of each event, however, such norms act as tools for problem solving. As the preceding illustrations show, the use of such tools requires skills, including these:

- An understanding of the rules of Black modes discourse and the roles of the participants within it
- An understanding of the positioning of the speaker as it shapes authorial intent
- Ability to identify implied audience
- The underlying meaning or intent of a text
- An understanding of coherence within inference generation
- Ability to generate response to claim within a narrative
- Ability to take on roles (and to step in and out of them within the discourse) through the appropriation of contextualized terms in order to construct an expert knowledge and enact an epistemic stance

Classroom discourse events, like those in the salon, are a kind of community of practice (Lave, 1996)—hybrid in nature, in which students and teachers collaborate to build on culturally and socially constructed academic knowledge toward the goal of dealing with problems in literary texts. And like the salon, this hybrid space is polycontextual, multivoiced, and multiscripted, a space within which students become expert learners as they wrestle with themes in texts as both local (near as in everyday events) and distal (far as in historical or global events), but not always collaborative, coordinated, and meaningful to their lives. Furthermore, individuals' potential to access and engage with cultural resources such as speaking, and arrangements such as performing, for the purposes of reasoning about particular kinds of social dilemmas outside the classroom is often either ignored or viewed as an obstacle to learning.

The kinds of practices found in most classroom communities of practice, particularly those in secondary language arts, center on the reading of texts—where individuals take up certain ideas and value systems in regard to written texts. A consideration of social readings, like those in the salon, can provide situated contexts for engaging youth, not only in traditional academic literacies, but in broader problem-posing and problem-solving strategies that extend beyond the classroom. In Chapter 5 we will examine more closely how, within the context of the salon, youth are socialized into structures of argumentation and social reading within Shoptalk as an instrument of problem solving. A consideration of such structures enables those interested in the social and academic development of all students, and those who are drawn particularly to the experiences of African American youth, to better account for the interplay between culture and context in learning.

CHAPTER 5

What Gets Read, Who Is the Reader, and How Do You Talk Back to Disempowering Texts?

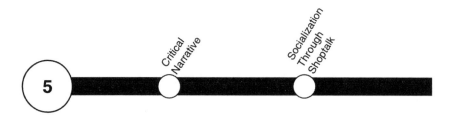

How, through Shoptalk, are youth able to consider alternative perspectives, take on roles within the argumentation, and digest (and even assume) multiple points of view—skills required in any language arts classroom?

Chapters 2 and 3 gave us a glimpse of how participants who are engaged in Shoptalk collaboratively construct what I have been calling narrative social texts. We learned that for cultural border crossers, like Darlene and Ms. Addie, to read a social text is to go beyond surface interpretation and to engage in a skillful reconstruction of that text in both action and consciousness. In doing so, participants of Shoptalk socially and orally produce something that is new and improvised, yet bears some clear relationship to the original text. I argued that these socially reconstructed oral texts become improvised, "rigged scripts,"—goal-oriented road maps within the discourse, offering participants alternative, sometimes-competing mechanisms for a kind of cultural consciousness, resiliency, and task-based problem solving. These rigged scripts also contribute to their belief systems about (and resistances to) competing ideologies and practices stressed in the official curriculum of the salon.

Using the lens of participatory appropriation, which directs our attention to ongoing development as people participate in events and thus handle subsequent events in ways based on their involvement in previous events (Rogoff, 1995), our focus will be on how participants of Shoptalk shift their thinking in ways that make a difference in subsequent events. We will draw our attention to the ways in which participants appear to reject seemingly status quo or prescribed formats, for engaging in a kind of literate problem solving that transforms their understandings regarding particular events. We will examine the structure of the argumentation that frames such problem solving. We also will explore how narrative texts are generated and open the door for certain outcomes (both good and bad) beyond those intended by the institutional script. In both events, the tools of Shoptalk become instruments of scaffolding one young participant into cultural practices, where she comes to consider alternative perspectives, take on roles within the argumentation, and digest (and even assume) multiple points of view in order to grapple with a personal dilemma.

The questions we will be asking ourselves along the way are:

- How do cultural norms for talk and participants' roles within the discourse contribute to the representation of teaching and learning?
- What structures of problem posing and problem solving do youth, as members of that culture, pick up and demonstrate within that context?
- What can we learn from participants' ability to navigate through the discourse and argumentative ability?

THE EMERGENCE OF A CRITICAL NARRATIVE TEXT

Let's begin by extending our analysis of Ms. Addie and the "problem in America." Recall that in Chapter 4, we considered both the receptive and productive aspects of Ms. Addie's narration of her cross-cultural encounter —both the reading and oral production of social texts. That discourse illuminated the following skills and features:

- Participants' social reading of an institutional (official) text and point of view
- Participants' ability to read the racialized subtext of the events and respond to them without buying into the assumptions of others
- Participants' unpacking and redefinition of the problem space
- Participants' introduction of an alternative cultural (unofficial) text and alternative point of view through rhetorical and discursive strategies

In what follows, we continue to eavesdrop on Ms. Addie and the other participants as they evaluate her experiences and interactions occurred outside the salon, in light of local notions of what is right, wrong, and just. As a participant moving across borders, Ms. Addie is acting in two social situations, neither of which includes members of the other group. Yet we see her reporting in a social situation that does not include members of both groups (Black and White) and around a topic directly related to ancestors of both groups (U.S. slavery). How she positions herself in relation to the other participants across contexts is key, therefore, and the positioning is carried out by this social actor by enacting multiple voices and identities, rather than taking up those imposed upon her. As the discussion continues, note how participants utilize Shoptalk as a means both for expressing and understanding who they are and for gaining access to implicit propositions about the self (Miller et al., 1990).

> *Ms. Addie:* Yes, yes. But you see this, this is a Black and White issue in this country and until people forgive. They have—we have to forgive them and they have to forgive themselves.
> *Wendi:* Acknowledge their wrongdoing.
> *Ms. Addie:* Acknowledge—that's exactly right.
> *Wendi:* And most of them are not going to do that.
> *Carmen:* And nobody's going to do that.
> *Ms. Addie:* Nobody's going to do that. I heard some stuff. And some of them look at me like, you know, "Why, why you doin' this?"
> *Wendi:* Why you doin' what?
> *Ms. Addie:* Why am I dressing like this?
> *Wendi:* Oh, yeah, they hate that.
> *Ms. Addie:* And then they come and I say, "My name is Harriet Tubman and I am a slave."

There are several important points regarding the above excerpt. First is the shifting of the "problem space" ("we have to forgive them and they have to forgive themselves"), in order to account for a redefinition of the initial problem: fear of talking/teaching about slavery. By shifting this space through extension of the problem, Ms. Addie and the other participants do more than introduce an unofficial point of view to the equation. By embodying the historical figure of Harriet Tubman, Ms. Addie once again repositions her role within the narrative in two important ways: (1) to that of a "functional text" in that she physically takes on the living embodiment of an important and historical textbook figure, and (2) as a kind of culture worker, as one who interprets the word and world and seeks the psychological, cultural, and physical liberation of Black people on all levels. She thus is serving in the West African tradition of Jali, who functioned as professional oral historians and storytellers and whose role in the African community was indispensable. Hale (2007) offers an elaborate "job description" for the Jali: historian, genealogist, advisor, spokesperson, diplomat, mediator, praise-singer, interpreter/translator, musician/composer, teacher, warrior, witness, and exhorter. Traditionally, a Jali operated in the service of royalty and frequently was tasked with recounting (via singing, praise poetry, etc.) events important to the ruling class. However, owing to historical changes over time (especially enslavement, colonization, African Diaspora, industrialization, urbanization), Jali took on more of a populist mission as their storytelling role expanded from performance to service and to other strata within the larger community. In fact, one of the critical skills of a Jali is her or his ability to improvise (Kazembe, 2012).

Today, the critical presence and function of the Jali take on expanded cultural, political, and ethical significance when considered alongside contemporary social and academic challenges confronting urban schools, literacy educators, African American students, and the wider Black community (Kazembe, 2012). We will see something similar occur when we examine events that take place in the classroom, as students attempt to "try on" the discourse of a particular text (Chapter 8) in order to make meaning of it.

Second, the co-construction of this critical social reading of race, gender, and social relations enables Ms. Addie to push hard against the boundaries between the official and the unofficial points of view by graying the lines between them. It is the redirection of the initial problem through narrative supports (which include AAE norms) that enables the co-construction of meaning and leads to a "critical reading" of gender, race, class, and social relations. This redirection homes in on what Ms. Addie finds salient about the problem, further contextualizing her character (Harriet Tubman) by the official point of view, "Why, why, you doin' this?"

It is at this point of indirection that a pivotal exchange occurs between the official points of view and the unofficial view in which Ms. Addie literally reads, within the African American discourse tradition, her embodied text as Harriet Tubman on the opposition. (For additional examples of this, see Majors, 2004.) The African American notion of reading as an interpretive practice also occurs through the process of "reading dialect," in which members of the African American community contrast or otherwise highlight obvious features of AAE in an unambiguous manner to make a point (Morgan, 1998).

This leads to the third point, which is that participants' roles within the discourse of Shoptalk also contribute to the construction of a paradigm surrounding interactional processes that asserts a community hierarchy of power and knowledge. For example, Ms. Addie's insistence that the real problem in America is fear of difference and lack of forgiveness challenges the assumptions of those she encounters. This places her in a position of power, in that she has the ability to alter those assumptions through her single response, which is to say, "I am Harriet Tubman." In Ms. Addie's utterances, "My name is Harriet Tubman and I am a slave," she aligns herself oppositionally with her audience, altering the interactional processes that assert a community hierarchy of power (White over Black) and knowledge (White over Black) within both contexts, and it is in the resolution of that dissonance that participants cultivate the ability to read different points of view.

Finally, it is important to note that Ms. Addie does not lose her cool; she simply contrasts her point of view and identity with those imposed upon her through an institutional point of view by this performative shift. The audience picks up on this shifting in the problem space through the prosodic shift. Ms. Addie takes on the prosodic structure of "I am a slave" narrative and calmly and matter-of-factly states the utterance gracefully. She reports her own speech in a situation where she acted coolly and in a manner that led to her point getting across in an optimally understated (yet direct) manner. She reports her speech to her salon audience, and perhaps to her White onlookers, very slowly, sweetly, and pointedly (in teacher-speak), with very varied pitch contour (up and down). She is showing her audience, in a sense socializing them to, the underlying tension of her message, which is to contest not only an ascribed positioning by the others but their resistance to the identity she constructs for herself, by contrasting the content with the way she says it. Her White onlookers may not have picked up on the distinction, but Ms. Addie knows, and the salon audience knows, that this is an act of resistance.

This particular act of resistance is conveyed through narrative meaning-making and allows for a simultaneous understanding of her own position as well as an understanding of her audience. Through a narrative "lens," Ms. Addie fictionalizes and reasserts an ideological positioning, creating a distinct voice that allows her some agency. The narrative serves the illocutionary function of a coping mechanism while at the same time creating an interpretive stance toward a phenomenon; both are part of Ms. Addie's procedural toolkit, allowing her to "endure the conflicts and contradictions that social life generates" (Bruner, 1990, p. 43).

In addition to repositioning her role within the discourses as a cultural border crosser, Ms. Addie utilizes multiple literacy tools, including functional and social readings of texts, in order to construct and move knowledge from one system (official) to another (unofficial) for the purposes of "critically" co-constructing new meanings. Such an intertextual reading is a skill performed by expert readers both within and outside classrooms.

Within the discourse, Ms. Addie and her interlocutors make use of not only their social reading skills, but their functional skills as well, invoking various texts such as the Bible and a historical book belonging to Ms. Addie. In doing so, Ms. Addie and the women re-appropriate what gets read and who gets to be the reader in contexts of problem solving. What emerges from that context is a narrative text, created by participants of Shoptalk, that both alters the problem situation as well as the assumptions and individual identities that inform it.

Ms. Addie: Me, I have this book that I was given when I went to the Newberry library for this program.

Audience: Mm-hmm.

Ms. Addie: Uh, they gave it the masters of the plantation when they got ready to die—here's the good part about this—they would write in their wills that "Sally May is freed upon my death."

Carmen: So, they would have a slave that they liked.

Ms. Addie: No, no, no, no, no! That's not the reason. Not 'cuz they like 'em so well. See, they were getting' ready to check out of this earth. And they, this was their way of sayin', "You know God, God is going to let me in."

Wendi: Ask him for a pardon, yeah.

Ms. Addie: But see, but see, they don't ask, they don't ask the people that they.

Carmen: Oh, not anybody ask the slave. Oh no.

Ms. Addie: Because they, they'd have to admit that you did something wrong.

Wendi: Exactly.

Ms. Addie: And, of course, you know, White folks can't admit they did anything wrong.

Wendi: That's right. That's exactly right.

Ms. Addie: So, they think, "I'll do this and God will let me on in." That's it.

Carmen: But see, what you saying is in the beginning, you all knew you were doin' wrong all the time. Yeah. You can never justify it, no matter what. No, you can't.

Ms. Addie: But see, God has already put everybody in.

Jackie: Can I say something? Can I make one point? I might be wrong, but White people think God is White. They think he's White. So, if you think that he's White, then you think that he's on your side. Did you ever notice in the gospels though? They never offer a description of his face in the natural.

Wendi: They think he's White.

Carmen: Isn't that something? Isn't that something? They think he's White.

Ms. Addie: Like Jackie said, like Jackie said, they still think that he's on their side.

Wendi: That's right.

This analysis of talk involving Ms. Addie is an attempt to substantiate two claims. The first is that talk in the hair salon is one among a number of resources available to participants as they negotiate emergent goals and construct identities for themselves. The norms for talk, artifacts, roles assumed, and the goals of each interact to constitute this workplace-community activity. Participants were presented through an analysis of multiple exchanges. These exchanges represent not only how, when, and where members classify and categorize events, objects, and one another in the context of the salon through a shared discourse, but also the subtle linguistic tools used by participants to both comply with and contest socially constructed identities.

FACILITATING SOCIALIZATION THROUGH SHOPTALK

We are nearing the end of our journey through the culturally shared and situated context of the salon. However, before we exit, I'd like to direct your attention to one last exchange, illustrating the ways in which Shoptalk, as a discourse, socialized adolescents within the salon into routine problem-solving strategies.

What follows examines how, through Shoptalk, youth were prompted to consider alternative perspectives, take on roles within the argumentation, and digest (and even assume) multiple points of view—skills that mimic those required in any language arts classroom. The event is one in which an adolescent mother presents a dilemma by making an official claim before an audience of adult men and women regarding her daughter's seeming failure to perform well at school. Undergirding this claim is the mother's account of an institutional (school) reading of her daughter's academic performance.

The mother's subsequent response, to send the child to live with her father, provokes an adult participant, who shows an interest in the young mother, along with other community members, to engage her in a little Shoptalk. It can be assumed that the adult participants of Shoptalk share a common set of experiences and mediational resources that prepare them to participate in local Shoptalk. However, it is the presence of the young women in this exchange, which propels the event forward, and enables participants to represent shared readings of the world through Shoptalk.

Jackie: Your daughter ready to get outta school?
Tramain: Yeah, but she gotta go right back to school anyway.
Jackie: Why she gotta go back?
Tramain: Summer school.
Jackie: They settin' her back?

Tramain: Uhm, hmm. 'Cause, uh. You know them tests, the Iowa Basic Test, but it's not called Iowa Basic Test in Catholic schools.

Carmen: It's called somethin' else?

Jackie: Yeah, right.

Tramain: Uhm, she, she, uhm, some of 'em she got below average.

Carmen: Uh-huh.

Tramain: And then some of her test she had was average. So, she wanna be below average, she goin' to summer school.

Carmen: She wanna be average?

Tramain: Naw, I'm sayin' she wanna be below average, I'm sendin' her back to summer school. 'Cause she know she can do better than that. So I told her. I said next year at this time If you don't do good in school, I'm takin' all her stuff and sendin' her to her daddy house.

Jackie: What, what are they called now?

Tramain: I don't know. Um.

Carmen: Standardized test.

Tramain: Yeah. But it's a different name in Catholic schools.

Carmen: Yeah, I know, right. You had 'em didn't you?

Tramain: Yeah, but it was Iowa Basic Test when I, when I was in, um, school. But they called something else in Catholic school. She just bein' lazy, so, she gotta go to summer school. And if she don't do good for next year—she get a warnin' grade.

Jackie: Uhm, hm.

Tramain: They already sent me a letter, they said if she do not do good next year that she will fail.

Jackie: Oh my, well how much, is her grades low, or what?

Tramain: She lazy. They know she can do it, but she just don't wanna do it. She want to do it when she get ready to.

Jackie: Is it just the test, or is it schoolwork too?

Tramain: Schoolwork too. So I told her. I said next year at this time, if you don't do good in school, I'm takin' all her stuff and sendin' her to her daddy house.

In the above exchange, we see the adult women's attempt to engage in Shoptalk when one of the women asks Tramain a question about her daughter, showing some interest in beginning a dialogue with Tramain. This serves as a prompt for the young mother and brings the topic of schooling to the floor. However, the general message here has to do with notions of care and helping the youth develop coping mechanisms that might enable her to respond differently, perhaps intellectually, to what she and they may view as threatening.

This mirrors what goes on in many mainstream classrooms where students are asked to respond to a text in ways that evoke a level of thoughtfulness and critical reflection. What is often absent from the traditional discourse of classrooms is a kind of pushback, or rather a space where multiple perspectives can be interrogated through cultural meanings and norms. Hence, to propel this interrogation, the women engage Tramain with the dilemma through a process of redirection in order to move the young mother into a different kind of problem solving, one that is dialogic and includes a subtle attention to and awareness of the subtext of the events.

Tramain responds to the women's interest in a dialogue, and one of the women asks interpolated questions, giving Tramain plenty of "talk room" to finish her thoughts. Another women, a stylist in the salon, questions Tramain and makes a request for more information, which propels the conversation forward, as more information is disseminated by Tramain.

> *Carmen:* Don't go to extremes!
> *Tramain:* Yes I am!
> *Jackie:* Don't get drastic now. Maybe she just need extra help?
> *Ms. Wanda:* I was thinkin' the same thing.
> *Tramain:* She gettin' it. She get tutorin'.
> *Ms. Wanda:* But maybe it's, sometimes you gotta kinda get—
> *Tramain:* No! She just lazy.
> *Carmen:* But you gotta be patient with her. She might not be lazy.
> *Ms. Wanda:* Yeah, you really do.

After a sufficient amount of information has been presented, Tramain makes a strong claim about her plans for her child to which one of the adult women states a judgment for the first time in the exchange when she says, "Don't go to extremes." She does this after a period of neutral, fact-based discussion driven mainly by Tramain. It would appear as though she is letting Tramain have her say before delivering an opinion on the matter. The opinion is mildly stated, but a third adult, Ms. Wanda, collaborates in the conversation by interjecting her concurring opinion. Thus, they align to offer the mentoring of an older, more experienced community of women.

> *Tramain:* No! She just lazy, y'all.
> *Ms. Wanda:* But you gotta be patient with her.
> *Carmen:* She might not be lazy, you might . . . [is interrupted]
> *Ms. Wanda:* Maybe you could help her more.
> *Tramain:* No, look. We already tested her to see if she was kinda slow,
>   to see if she had dyslexia, you know, stuff like that she already been

tested for. Catherine do not have no disability. The only disability she have is bein' lazy.

Carmen: Now, it might not be lazy, it might be she not graspin' it.

Ms. Wanda: Sometimes when they, yeah, I was gone say, now sometimes when they don't understand, you lookin' at it and it look like they being lazy but they really embarrassed to say, "I don't understand."

Carmen: Right.

Tramain: But see, she . . .

Carmen: I had that problem one time when I was in 3rd grade when we started doin' fractions, I couldn't grasp it.

Tramain: But Catherine, if she sittin' in front of me she can do it. But if she at school she don't wanna do it. It's like she daydreaming.

Ms. Wanda: But you know sometimes, like, my son went through periods where he wasn't doin' as well as I thought he should do and I found, I had to keep on it 'til I found somethin' to motivate him, to make him do it, and I found out that you know he's a boy, since he's a boy, boys like competition, I got a egg timer and he liked to race against the clock. That made him start doin' work at a different level. He, you know it started makin' it fun for him to have that challenge to be able to do in a certain amount of time.

Tramain: So you.

Ms. Wanda: And that's what sparked him to start doin' better. I'd say, "OK, you got 15 minutes to do your English," you know, and then he, uh, say, "OK, well, you know set the clock. I'm ready." You know, and he would not rush and make it, uh, you know, it was good work.

Tramain: Uhm, hmmm.

Ms. Wanda: He just liked competition. So that's the way you, I got him an egg timer.

Jackie: 'Cause it kept, it kept his mind stimulated.

Wendi: It kept him more interested, right?

Tramain: But she got . . .

Ms. Wanda: But when I just let him take as much time, he just be lookin' in space.

Tramain: Right. That's what I'm saying.

Ms. Wanda: Doin' this, and ballin' up paper and sharpenin' pencils.

Carmen: It might be a little simple thing, you know.

Tramain rebuts lamely ("She got tutors") and Ms. Wanda gives a directive for Tramain not to go to "extremes." Tramain now has been "talked" to and becomes excited. She exclaims her right to go to extremes quite loudly, and Ms. Wanda, in a calm tone reasserts that Tramain should calm down. In making such a request, the women are not attempting to control Tramain; neither are they directly calling attention to Tramain's tone in terms of how her message is being delivered. Rather, in issuing the directive, what is being elicited from Tramain is recognition of the importance that she take note of what she is saying. The women appear to recognize that there is an underlying tension in Tramain's message and accordingly they lay the groundwork for Tramain to recognize what they already have—that there are other texts, other scripts to consider.

Additionally, the women are socializing Tramain into a very complex way by which to respond to official texts, in that they are calling on her to reposition herself in much the same way that we saw both Darlene and Ms. Addie do when they reported their own speech coolly and in a manner that ultimately led each adult to getting her point across in an optimally understated (yet direct) manner. This, in turn, enabled each woman to contest not only an ascribed positioning by the others but their resistance to the identity she constructed for herself, by contrasting the content with the way she said it. As each adult woman above latches/caps the other's exchange, they exert their right to tell Tramain how it is, but do so respectfully and without excessive emotion, not deviating from the intended goal. As members of a group that historically has been denied social power, the adult women are modeling the understanding of when and where to display such readings, and when and where to keep them subterfuged—a skill that may be important for survival.

In the above exchange, adult participants of Shoptalk use both their individual and collective readings to challenge the *content and the form of reasoning process* of the adolescent mother. In this context, both the readings of events (framed by the claim posited by Tramain) and the counter-readings (offered by the adults) function as tools for socializing Tramain into alternative readings, and hence alternative points of view of that official text. For example, during the exchange, Tramain is given more time to develop the topic, which is still about her daughter. One of the adult women then relates her past similar experience through narrative, and another woman follows suit when given an in and discusses her strategy when her son experienced a situation similar to that of Tramain's daughter. This brings an alternative point of view or text to the floor, one intended for Tramain to consider, but to no avail.

> *Tramain:* But she got competition. 'Cause her, uh.
> *Ms. Wanda:* But it may, hers may not be competition. It could be somethin' else. But you gotta kinda keep tryin'.

Wendi: Right, don't give up.
Tramain: I'm not given up. I ain't given up.
Wendi: Don't send her off to her daddy.

Despite Tramain's status as a youth, she was the original narrator of
the topic, so she remains the focus, despite the other women's position of
offering advice and co-constructing. The other two women suggest possible
sources for the child's problem at school; however, Tramain remains on the
defensive. This topic continues until the issue of a new tutor as a solution
arises.

Tramain: I think that's what I'mma do though. . . . 'Cause she not, I
    don't think that she's actually graspin' everything she supposed to
    do.
Jackie: You ever talk to her about it? Just ask her plain out?
Tramain: Mm-hmm.
Jackie: You know what's going on?
Tramain: Yeah.
Jackie: What your daughter say?
Tramain: She said, that, uh, like I talked to her about daydreaming.
Jackie: Mm-hmm.
Tramain: During class and stuff, but she just like, "Don't know why I
    do it." I even had her father try to talk to her to see why she does it.
    I mean, I used to daydream when I was in school, you know, that's
    what kids do. I mean, all kids daydream in school at some point.
Jackie: Uhm, hmm.
Tramain: But it's affectin' now that it's affectin' her work.
Jackie: Right?
Tramain: So you know? That's what I'm talkin' about.
Jackie: Uhm, uhm.
Tramain: I'm not gone pack her stuff up and send her on down there.
Jackie: Right.
Tramain: I just try to scare her.
Jackie: Well, that's not a good idea.
Tramain: So she can, uh, so she can try to start improvin'.
Jackie: Yeah.
Tramain: 'Cause her daddy just let her do whatever she wanna do.
Jackie: Well, then, how is that gone work then? If he gonna let her do
    what she wanna do?
Tramain: I'm just tryin' to scare her.
Jackie: But that ain't gone work. Now, we gotta come up with another
    plan.

Tramain: I'm going to try and get her some more help though, for next
   year.

In the above excerpt, all participants develop this topic, interjecting
their own relevant stories and opinions. Together, Jackie, Carmen, Wendi,
and Ms. Wanda suggest that perhaps Tramain's daughter's problem has a
cause outside the curriculum at school (i.e., her failure to grasp certain concepts), but suggest this without stepping on, or "downing," Tramain. Then
Ms. Wanda relates her similar experience, putting her "past self" on the
same level as Tramain, further engendering solidarity and connection. In
making herself vulnerable for the purposes of problem solving, Ms. Wanda
makes a culturally responsive, pedagogical move. Such a move is characterized through the use of personal narrative in which the adult (teacher) attempts to make a connection (through sharing of a personal detail) between
the learner and some shared experience in an effort to close the gap between
spaces of knowing that might separate them.
   This is accomplished not through the maintenance of distance and objectivity, as would be seen in traditional classroom instruction and its supporting research, but through quite the opposite in that it is reflexive, liberatory,
and dialogic, embracing both the local (near to) and the distal (far from).
Narrations of understanding, like that shared by Ms. Wanda, lend themselves to a kind of discourse that is noted in spaces of teaching and learning
that are culturally shared and situated. This kind of discourse affirms certain
behaviors, attitudes, and performances of all those in the event as being culturally shared, productive, and meaningful and valued.
   Tramain conveys that she's heard enough in a tone belying her discon-
tent as Jackie reasserts that she's not trying to down her. By saying this,
Jackie shows that she is aware of and attentive to Tramain's conversational
needs. This might be especially the case, because Ms. Wanda and Jackie
seem to truly care about Tramain's daughter's situation and want their advice to be heard and considered, which would not be as likely if they of-
fended Tramain.
   At this point in the conversation, Ms. Wanda stresses that Tramain cannot give up. For the first time, speaker Wendi (one of the hairdressers) has
an active part in the conversation, and she follows the previously established
pattern of turn taking and tone of advice giving. Jackie even incorporates
Wendi's comments into her speech. This excerpt shows women closely attentive to one another's conversational needs (time to talk), right to make/
defend a point, and react to and build off of one another's content and mode
of discourse. Emotional tone and pitch/cadence are respected as a meta-
language, as shown by the other women's supportive responses to Tramain's
frustration. They do not coddle her, though, and assert their opinion about

how she should deal with her daughter's dilemma. It seems that they are concerned that her plans are inappropriate and attempt to intervene to help the situation.

The other women support Tramain and urge her to take control of the situation. They are firm about this advice, and speech overlaps, showing heightened involvement with the topic. This topic surfaces again, and the women collaborate heavily by building off of one another's phrase structure and closely latching their comments. The end of the conversation shows the women incorporating themes (the daddy's house is a bad idea, no one wants to disrespect anyone else, try another tutor, don't scare Catherine), increasing the rate of exchange, and decreasing talk time. The overall map of the conversation regarding topic development is as follows:

Official Script—Tramain's daughter's progress at school
Initiated by Jackie
Developed mainly by Tramain
Jackie makes assessment/Carmen enters
All three overlap and Jackie/Carmen relate personal experiences to develop topic

Unofficial Script—Possibility of hiring new tutor to help situation
Initiated by Jackie
Developed mainly by Ms. Wanda
Tramain is on the defensive, but works within others' suggestions to find solution
Entrance of speaker Wendi
Topic switches when Tramain becomes aggravated

Rigged Script—Possible sources of Catherine's distraction
Initiated by Tramain
Developed mainly by Ms. Wanda and Jackie
Other women support Tramain and urge her to take charge of situation
They collaborate on pros and cons of different solutions discussed thus far

WHAT HAVE WE LEARNED?

The above illustration shows participants of Shoptalk actively engaged in the processes of socialization through their *direct participation* in this mode of reasoning. This chapter takes a critical look at cultural socialization as an event in learning. Cultural socialization is a community-based social practice through which members, in oral exchanges, convey certain ideas and value systems with regard to how to see the world and oneself within it. Such a practice can involve structures of problem posing and problem solving that youth, as members of that culture, are able to pick up and demonstrate within and across contexts. This view frames, in part, how we account for (1) the role of African American cultural-community processes for reasoning through life's dilemmas, and (2) how the classroom can be transformed into a robust space where students may apply such processes to their academic and lived lives. Shoptalk is a framework for a process of cultural socialization that draws on community practices for problem solving and development. In Chapter 6, we will examine how cultural socialization can serve as a useful tool not only in community but in classroom practices.

Little qualitative attention, however, has been given to community social spaces and networks outside the family, which offer structures of cultural socialization that shape and frame reasoning. Far less is understood about how, through participation within such networks, individuals acquire tools for problem posing and problem solving within academic contexts. For the most part, research on reasoning has been highly reductionist, both theoretically and methodologically (Kuhn, 1991). These reductionist models do not account for language and culture, but rather attempt to isolate reasoning, "focusing on deductive (general to particular, syllogistic reasoning) rather that inductive (open-ended reasoning that draws general conclusions), for example" (p. 32).

As an alternative to such models, research that occurs in cultural-community settings takes on the nuances of the everyday and those complicating factors of problem posing and problem solving that are a part of being human. From this perspective, and with regard to problem-solving processes within oral discourses, "there are no definitively correct answers, the number and kinds of possible responses are open ended, and the information an individual can bring to bear on the problem is similarly unconstrained" (Kuhn, 1991, p. 40). Cultural-community practices, those which socialize adolescents into such processes, offer a real-world view of the cognitive tools individuals within cultures bring to bear on knowledge construction, complex ideas that depend on linguistic expression, and higher-order thinking and reasoning.

Throughout this and previous chapters, the speakers have demonstrated:

- How culturally shared interactional norms, evident and situated within the hair salon, inform knowledge building

- How participant's roles as social actors contribute to the representations of African American English discourse
- How discourse norms provide participation structures that invite engagement within complex problem-solving tasks

They have demonstrated, in part, how language and culture interact to inform learning and teaching in a community setting, how knowing and teaching are linked to context, how context is linked to identity, and how discourse features that characterize membership in the setting of the hair salon provide meaningful opportunities for participation.

The mutual understanding of the speech genre of Shoptalk creates roles for those who understand the talk, and these roles provide opportunities for arguments and narratives to be co-constructed toward socially meaningful goals. These goals, in the workplace setting of the hair salon, have both social and cognitive dimensions. The cognitive dimensions have to do with figuring out how to produce evidence that propels the narrative or argument forward. The social dimensions have to do with seeing oneself as a productive participant, having an identity as a member of the group, and the reinforcement of one's identity. This cognitive and social collaboration can be negotiated through apprenticeship and guided participation because members, both experts (Darlene) and novices (interns and clients), share an understanding of the norms for who can talk, about what, and how in these semiotic spaces.

Central to the active changes involved in this particular speech event is the appropriation of understandings by individual participants. According to Rogoff (1995), the term *appropriation* refers to the change resulting from a person's own participation in an activity, participation that involves creative efforts to understand and contribute to it. Such efforts involve bridging between competing ways of understanding a situation. Communication and shared efforts always involve adjustments between participants to stretch their common understanding to fit with *new perspectives* in the shared endeavor.

IMPLICATIONS FOR SCHOOLING

In addition to providing supports to thinking, such tools function as part of a transformative framework for students and education. According to Banks (1998, 2001, 2003), aims of the transformative approach to education are to teach students to think critically and to develop the skills to formulate, document, and justify their conclusions. Such an approach affords students opportunities to engage in critical thinking and to develop more reflective perspectives about what they are learning. The approach pushes students to look critically and reflectively as they examine issues both inside and outside the classroom.

In education, our understanding of the developmental sources and pathways of youth thinking and socialization has expanded in the past 2 decades. Several features of this knowledge growth are especially salient. First, as in many other areas of developmental and educational sciences, psychology has gained an appreciation for context in the development of adolescent thinking. A second phenomenon, according to Keating and Sasse (1996), is the growing recognition of the effect of noncognitive features of adolescent development on the growth of thinking. For example, the role of social relationships increasingly is seen as central to the understanding of cognitive development throughout the life span, and adolescence is no different in that respect. A third trend is to take account of the essential contextualization and developmental integration by embedding core research questions in more real-world or applied contexts (Keating & Sasse, 1996). One way of capturing the central tendency of these salient features is to identify and explore critical processes during the adolescent years.

CHAPTER 6

Shifting Borders and Landscapes

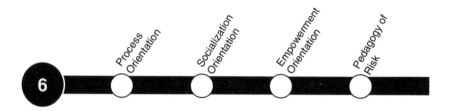

What shifts in paradigms must we make in order to cross borders of classroom and community?

With transfers in hand, it is important before we board our next train to reflect on the observations at our previous stops. As with all progress from one point to another, what we know of the past greatly influences how we experience what is to come. For example, we have spent time examining the structures, tools, norms, and conditions for talk that occur in the culturally shared community setting of the African American hair salon. When viewed through the conceptual lens of Shoptalk (see Chapter 2), talk in the salon can be seen as a kind of discourse, adhering to a set of assumptions, conditions, ideologies, and scripts. Individuals who engage in the discourse of Shoptalk take up participatory roles as social actors, often for purposes of instruction, which results in a transformation of the problem as well as participants' view of it.

We've seen how instruction is mediated through the discourse of social actors for particular purposes when taking into account Rogoff's *three planes of analysis* (Rogoff, 1995) as an analytical lens through which to view the activities that take place in the salon and, by extension, the classroom. Each purpose bears in mind a particular orientation—assumptions, shifting habits of mind, and procedural rules toward a given task. There are three orientations accounted for here: process, product, and socialization. The *process orientation* activity, at times, has been for the purpose of teaching a process or a particular task, and providing instruction through conversation in everyday situations where directives are embedded in the talk. For example, a client (as novice in the arena of hairstyling) may inquire as to the best way to style his or her hair, and the stylist (as expert) might respond with a series of steps the client can take to achieve that particular style. Here the stylist, as instructor, uses talk to convey certain procedures pertaining to hair care. Steps of a task are presented in a logical order according to hierarchy. The client, as student, listens to and observes how the steps are executed, with the intent of reproducing them and achieving a particular outcome.

Shifting from one plane to another enables us to keep this process orientation in the background, while zooming in on another. Therefore, in addition to this process orientation, instruction in the salon can take on a kind of *product orientation* as well. Here, the target of instruction is improved employee performance. However, the explicit end goal is not to psychoanalyze clients by way of expertise and psychosocial interaction through talk, but rather because it is a good business practice. As we saw in our earlier stop into Posh Salon, for example, in documenting the forms of guided participation, we are able to identify the interactions and supports that employers and employees provide to one another, in conjunction with the use of artifacts of apprenticeship, such as institutional curriculum and narrative imaginings. I think of an apprenticeship as providing conceptual affordances. That is, in an apprenticeship one inherits a set of ways of thinking about a practice that generations before have found useful and productive. Participation in the practice also lends itself to extending the problem-solving tools across time. In this way, through participation, one inherits, appropriates, and expands the problem-solving tools available to the practice (Lee & Majors, 2003).

But as we saw in Chapter 3, the formalized institutional view for instruction is not always aligned with what or how something actually is learned, or even what may be considered useful by the learner for producing particular outcomes. For example, the formalized, institutional practices of management that framed teaching and learning in Posh Salon often did not account for informal overlap in systems of activity and the interwoven nature of human social practice surrounding the interactions of employees, which includes narrative storytelling as a mediational tool in problem solving. This is particularly important to note, as contexts for learning (which include the workplace as well as the classroom) are immanently hybrid: polycontextual, multivoiced, and multiscripted. As we saw in the workplace development of Rahla (John's employee), apprenticeship into practice was a hybrid space of problem solving, collaboration, cooperation, and deviation. In other words, productive development may be the result of not only cooperation, but also kinds of tensions, deviance from norms, conflicts, and resolutions that lend themselves to learning. We will consider this important aspect of sociocultural activity later in this chapter as it informs the learning context, through the Shoptalk model, in the secondary language arts classroom.

Before moving on, however, another view of instruction is worth mentioning here as it, too, will inform how we experience the Shoptalk classroom. This view has to do with a kind of *socialization orientation* to instruction. A view of activity within the hair salon enabled me as researcher to focus my attention on the "system of interpersonal engagements and arrangements" contributing to the sociocultural processes of knowledge building (Rogoff, 1995, p. 146). Such interpersonal engagements and arrangements involved clients and stylists as social actors (Goffman, 1981) who brought to their interactions shared cultural and social norms for participation: rules, values, goals, and mediating artifacts (such as AAE talk). These shared cultural and social norms determined the participants' interactions with other members of the activity. Through guided participation in specific problem solving, Shoptalk can socialize adolescents/young adults into routine problem-solving strategies. As we saw in Chapter 5, older adults, using narrative, collaboratively took up and redirected these dilemmas in nonthreatening ways that afforded multiple perspectives for the challenged young mother.

The cognitive reasoning skills required of these participants to both construct and interpret such perspectives are akin to those required of interpretive tasks in the domain of literary response. That is, the adolescent/young adult is socialized into (1) a participatory role within the argumentative discourse that includes African American norms and values; (2) a process of reasoning that involves an examination of multiple and often divergent perspectives that are applicable within and across other contexts; and (3) a culturally shared, interactive form of reasoned argumentation and problem solving that is both socially and cognitively beneficial. Older adults in salons assisted adolescents/young adults in developing routine, problem-solving strategies to deal with a range of personal dilemmas (e.g., responses to racist aggression, poverty, early teen pregnancies, education, law, religion).

Across each of these orientations to teaching and learning, the everyday, practical import of Shoptalk discourse has been of particular interest. We look to how Shoptalk participants tackle challenges in their day-to-day lives, whether within the workplace or beyond, and the ways that run counter to the broader society's view of what gets read and interpreted, who is the reader, and how we talk back to disempowering texts and/or events. Let's call this an *empowerment through social reading orientation* to instruction.

In observations across multiple salons, we've seen how complex problem solving is linked to context, context is linked to identity, and discourse that characterizes membership within the group provides opportunities for participation in problem-solving tasks. Shoptalk participants have opportunities to question, challenge, and reconstruct knowledge, as well as transmit understandings of the world through such verbal strategies as participation, collaboration, and negotiation (Banks, 2001; Jacobs-Huey, 2006; Majors, 2003, 2004, 2007). Therefore, several assumptions have been made with regard to the instructional potential of the Shoptalk discourse. These include:

- Individuals collectively draw on a repertoire of literate practices that includes social reading, narrative imagining, and rigging to think, reason, and problem-solve within and across contexts (e.g., the reading of social relations)
- Individuals' cultural border-crossing experiences demonstrate the permeability of contexts with regard to literacy skill acquisition and use
- Structures of argumentation are culturally and situationally bound
- Narrative and culturally dialogic argumentation can aid in acts of resistance to socially imposed identities

Our train approaches now. As we strategically shift our placement on the platform in anticipation of where the doors will open, we must watch our steps, bearing in mind that "understanding the processes [of engagement] that become the focus of examination at each plane of analysis (community/institutional, interpersonal and personal) relies on understanding the processes in the background as well as those in the foreground of the analysis" (Rogoff, 1995, p. 148). If we can better understand how transformations occur for the participants, respective to all planes of our analysis, we might come to better understand teaching and learning in culturally shared and situated activity—Shoptalk.

In extending our discussion of cultural discourse beyond the salon, our geographic paradigm shifts so that we are crossing social and structural borders of race, culture, and social class—borders marked by space, time, and Chicago's complex history of attending to them both. We will recognize these borders, perhaps scrutinizing them as we survey the shifting stories and landscape—from golden Magnificent Mile, past the robust display of Puerto Rican heritage in Humboldt Park, and into the historic Lawndale community where a kind of teaching and learning awaits. This geographical straight shot from the hair salon to the community surrounding my classroom is an ideologically bumpy journey.

SHIFTING LANDSCAPES AND THE RESPONSE TO CHANGE

Known as "Chicago Jerusalem" in the 1920s and still recognized as "an archive of early 20th century American architecture"(Kozol, 2012), the Lawndale community rose to national prominence as the once-world headquarters for Sears, Roebuck and Company (http://tours.architecture. org/images/media/pdf/lawndale_factsheet.pdf). During the 2nd decade of the 20th century, Russian Jews became North Lawndale's largest residential group. Although not reaching the economic heights of the city's German Jews, North Lawndale's burgeoning population established its own small city of community institutions, including Mt. Sinai Hospital, Herzl Junior College (now Malcolm X College), several bathhouses, and a commercial strip on Roosevelt Road. One study found that in 1946 North Lawndale housed about 65,000 Jews, approximately one-quarter of the city's Jewish population.

Fourteen years later, however, 91% of the neighborhood residents were Black. Beginning in the 1950s, African Americans were moving into North Lawndale; some came from the South, others were displaced from their South Side homes by urban renewal projects. White residents, in turn, moved north to neighborhoods such as Rogers Park. Despite residential overcrowding, no new private housing was built in North Lawndale, and its physical decline increased to the point that the city's Community Conservation Board eventually recognized it as a conservation area (Encyclopedia of Chicago, 2005, http://www.encyclopedia.chicagohistory.org/pages/901.html).

In contrast to previous residents of North Lawndale, most new Black residents could not find work in the neighborhood. North Lawndale's industries now employed people who commuted to the neighborhood only for work. Consequently, the local consumer base became much poorer, and tensions grew between the Whites who worked in North Lawndale during the day and the Blacks who lived there. In 1966, the neighborhood's poverty prompted Martin Luther King, Jr., to pick North Lawndale as the base for the northern civil rights movement. Residents found King's visit highly symbolic: His stay attracted much attention, but little tangible change. In 1968, following the news of King's assassination, fires resulting from riots "consumed vital businesses and burned the neighborhood's economic fiber forever (Fountain & Rudd, 1992). Today,

> Vacant lots dot the West Side landscape. The glimmering neon signs that once lit up the promise of deals and steals now advertise Jesus at dozens of storefront churches. . . . A food desert today, lined with dimly [lit?] groceries that have

replaced bustling supermarkets. There is an endless stretch of liquor stores their faithful clientele lingering from dawn to dusk on the doorsteps sipping their daily sedative. Anger and frustration look over this mostly African-American community, in the same way as the billowing smoke of the 1968 riots. Tied deeply into that anger is the feeling among people left jobless, perhaps homeless, almost always hopeless that they have no ownership—not of their homes, and stores, not of their own destiny, not even of their dreams.

Given the changes that have occurred in the physical and social landscape, instructors like Ms. Addie as well as I find that we are positioned on the borders between social class cultural groups and discourse communities. Traversing these borders involves an acknowledgment and understanding of how individuals are both positioned by and participants of multiple (institutional) discourse communities. Our social readings of race, class, and gender become a demonstration of the permeability of social contexts. Instruction becomes the deliberate use of psychological, cultural, communal, and linguistic tools available to us via the Shoptalk pedagogical toolkit. Thus, instructors employing Shoptalk illuminate the tensions between dominant and nondominant cultural groups through a revoicing of what is deemed to be the official perspective in a particular discourse community. It is this social reading, demonstrating understandings of multiple perspectives, that characterizes teacher as the cultural border crosser.

LEARNING TO CROSS BORDERS

It looks like our stop is near. Before we get off the train, a certain shifting of mind is in order through a loosening of the restrictiveness of our mental seat belts, which enable us to maintain long-held ideologies, beliefs, and attitudes regarding the standards of humanity often attached to people of color. As we do so, we will not engage in a color-blind (blind to color) sidestep within the issue of critical discourse. Neither will we be blind to the "educative aspects of anger and frustration," both of which are "necessary for a beneficial and truly liberatory dialogue" on critical race pedagogy to take place (Leonardo & Porter 2010, p. 153). In accepting this stance, we must, as Leonardo and Porter suggest:

> undo the violence that is inherent in safe-space dialogue, and . . . enact a form of liberatory violence within race discussions to allow for a creativity that shifts the standards of humanity. In other words, anger, hostility, frustration, and pain are characteristics that are not to be avoided under the banner of safety, which only produces Freire's (1993) "culture of silence." They are attributes that are to be recognized on the part of both whites and people of color in order to

engage in a process that is creative enough to establish new forms of social exis-
tence, where both parties are transformed. That is not a form of violence that is
life threatening and narcissistic, but one that is life affirming through its ability
to promote mutual recognition. (p. 149)

My students and I in the high school classroom where I put Shoptalk
into instructional practice bear some similarity as border crossers. I, like
many of them, was raised in this community and share not only the historical legacy described above, but its cultural antecedents, access to formal and
informal networks, traditions, and epistemology grounded in community-
based cultural socialization practices. Such networks provide access to messages containing political and cultural themes that run counter to those in
dominant society. At times such themes are construed as highly provocative,
volatile, and controversial (especially by non-Blacks). Those who write/re-
cite in this vein employ the pedagogical stagecraft tools of emotional appeal,
projection, theatricality, and metaphorical emphasis within narrative to represent, reflect, and articulate information and ideas using artistic means (Kazembe, unpublished doctoral dissertation).

My youth bore witness to this kind of cultural brokering in a time
when this community (or at least my memory of it) appeared vital and
full of promise. Around me, stories came to life right before my eyes, and
I was called on to create an imagined background for them. These were
stories of our parents' childhood at a time when African Americans were
colored and a loaf of bread cost a dime. People I'd never met would be
resurrected and bit by bit pieced together with the enchanted details for
my mind's eye.

From my mother's lips, strangers were made familiar and given the breath
of life in words and gestures that shaped, colored, and made their meanings—meanings that played out in a scenery long since decayed. For long
afternoons through late evenings, we'd sit, listen, and learn. In my mind these
experiences were what brought us together as a unified whole and made us
a family, a community. However, they were also what separated us from the
rest of the world. "Flickering images on television shows" (Gates, 1994, p.
20) gave me glimpses of life in another world, a world of *Happy Days, My
Three Sons, The Brady Bunch*, and countless other "middle-class Whites who
looked, lived and sounded nothing like us" (Gates, 1994, p. 21).

Fillmore (1991) comments that:

Language minority children are aware that they are different the moment they
step out of their homes and into the world of school. They do not even have
to step out of the house. They have only to turn on the television and they can
see that they are different in language, in appearance and in behavior, and they
come to regard these differences as undesirable. (p. 342)

As the "invisible culture" (Erickson & Mohatt, 1982, p. 136) of White folks opened up to my eyes, the meaning of the world no longer emerged singularly as melodic sounds cascading off the tips of Black folks' tongues on porches and in kitchens, but rather as cashmere sweaters, pearls, powdered faces, and straight hair. Power didn't sit on porches because as I had imagined, White folks had special rooms made just for that purpose. And most of all, power never said *ain't*, or cursed, or knew how to do the Watusi way back in the day. As Delpit (1995) suggests, power, or rather "the culture of power" (p. 24), was something that, if you were not already a "participant," somehow you'd better learn the rules for, just in case.

Talk had boundaries and rules that included more than identifiable types of linguistic discourse. Who was talkin', who was listenin', and where they were at were equally as important as how they were sayin' it. This linguistic system comprises more than just a "uniform grammar" (Labov, 1972, p. 174). What is more than "its phonology, syntax, tense and aspect systems, and lexical semantics" (p. 174), is what it carries on its linguistic back—the values, beliefs, understandings, wisdom, and traditions. It is that talk which is ultimately the "crucial link between parents and children," (Fillmore, 1991, p. 343), between the member and the community. It is the talk through which meaning and culture are imparted.

For several years, my early education took place in Lawndale schools. Edison Elementary School, a short walk from my grandmother's porch, would be the final stop for a group of promenading schoolchildren whose kinky resistance also was combed straight each morning. Here, we lifted our voices each morning to James Weldon Johnson's Negro Anthem after reciting a Pledge of Allegiance to the flag. Nearly all of the teachers were Afro-wearing community members, committed not only to teaching our minds but to nurturing our intellect so that we could become what we chose.

As a student in this community, what I learned to understand was that I had a place in the world of words—written and spoken. The possibility that was mine in voice came through reading—after feeling the soft, red clay of the country roads between my toes, while playing barefoot with Maya Angelou, when she was a young Marguerite Johnson, and together we discovered why the caged bird sings. Yet, my greatest discovery in books was that others existed whose lives were bound not only in print, but in the same Black body as my own. Not just reading—I was digesting, and page after page I could ease my hunger, my desire, my obligation to be fed and to grow into the voice my eyes discovered. Yet, it was imperative to read between the lines of characters expressing thoughts and opinions about race, whether conservative or progressive, and attach to whatever spoke to me. In her essay entitled "Learning Past the Hate," hooks (2010) speaks of reading a novel by her beloved William Faulkner. In her essay, she states that it "would have been a tremendous loss to [her] construction of self and identity if [she] had refused to read Faulkner because he was racist and sexist" (p. 108), as she felt a love and attachment for the character of the South, the setting of his works.

As students and sharers in the community, we all learned early on that "a devotion to learning, to a life of the mind, was a counter-hegemonic act" (hooks, 1994, p. 2), a fundamental way to resist power. Although they didn't name those terms, my teachers were "enacting a revolutionary pedagogy of resistance" (p. 2) by deeming us Black children exceptional, gifted, talented. These teachers worked for us, and, more important, with us, to ensure that we could fulfill our intellectual destiny. In the classroom of my youth, students were encouraged to talk and to think critically with regard to texts, while confronting negative and positive images of their community and of themselves. Just as the hair salon serves as a safe space where members of the community come to "skillfully deflect the psychological attacks" that come with being human in an Othered body (Hill-Collins, 2000, p. 46), teachers worked with us to create the kind of space where we:

- Understood what we were to do
- Were able to develop meaningful goals we could not achieve on their own
- Were able to take risks and learn meaningful tasks
- Saw the work we did as relevant to some goals

Hence, they knew us, they were us, and in their eyes I saw that they loved me, despite the fact that my presence was absent from the world's view. Many of my teachers, particularly those who were members of the community, recognized and understood this absence and sought to prepare us, directly and indirectly, for the challenges of the road ahead.

Hughes and Chen (1999) categorize racial socialization messages as focusing on (1) an emphasis of cultural heritage and pride, or "cultural socialization"; (2) "preparation for future bias"; (3) "promoting racial mistrust"; and (4) "egalitarianism" (p. 473). They point out that these messages can be synergistic, verbal or nonverbal, deliberative or unintended, and proactive or reactive (Coard et al., 2004, p. 280). In their investigations, Stevenson and colleagues (2002) found that protective factors among African American youth they researched include alertness to discrimination and coping with antagonism. Proactive factors include cultural pride reinforcement and cultural legacy appreciation. Mainstream socialization is seen as neutral and not either protective or reactive practice, but still quite important in understanding the complexity of racial socialization communications.

Such messages are a part of people's cultural ways of knowing, which enable them to deal with, cope with, and handle the not-so-invisible aggressions of daily life, and the social, economic, structural, and scientific influences that produce them. Accordingly, thinking, learning, and teaching are part of the complex processes of socialization within the classroom. Consequently, it is important to make explicit the socializing mechanisms that otherwise are eclipsed within traditional academic settings. Chapter 8 elaborates upon these complex processes and the ways in which they are made explicit through academic practices.

PEDAGOGY OF RISK

One last word of caution before we reach our destination, where we briefly will explore classroom activity as an instance of Shoptalk. Elsewhere I've argued that the urban classroom provides a unique context to explore the hierarchical nature of race relations (Majors & Ansari, 2009). Unfortunately, there is a "color-blind" or "safe" discourse that does not nurture any exploration of this phenomenon. As Leonardo and Porter (2010) remind us, it is common to put the condition of "safety" around public race dialogue as a procedural rule in education. Like brackets, such a condition maintains "comfort zones" while at the same time inflicting what is a persistent and symbolic form of violence experienced by people of color (p. 139). The question (or rather the elephant in the room) remains, safe to whom? According to the authors, "A subtle, but fundamental violence (silence) is enacted in safe discourses, which must be challenged through a pedagogy of disruption" (p. 139), one that includes *risk discourse*: "Risk discourse is in itself a form of violence, but a humanizing rather than repressive one that does not assume safety, but does include contradictions and tension" (p. 139).

Part of color-blindedness is to demand that race dialogue take place in a safe environment. This is tantamount to premising racial pedagogy on assumptions about comfort, which quickly degrade antiracist teaching into image and personal management (A. Thompson, 2003). As opposed to this, critical race pedagogy is inherently risky, uncomfortable, and fundamentally unsafe (Lynn, 1999), particularly for Whites. This does not equate with creating a hostile situation, but acknowledges that pedagogies that tackle racial power will be most uncomfortable for those who benefit from that power.

It is important, therefore, that we first acknowledge such discomfort here, as exploring these complicated and nuanced issues of culture, class, and racial identity is an essential precursor to understanding literacy and learning in contexts where people of color reside. This imperative becomes increasingly clear as both the insistence on color-blindness enacted through a kind of safe discourse (one that assumes safety for Whites) *and* the racial divide continue to grow simultaneously between teacher and student in the urban classroom.

Second, in not paying attention to difference, teachers do a disservice to their instruction and the students they teach in that (1) they minimize the experiences of their students, and (2) they privilege their own cultural and intellectual practices over the lived experiences of their students. This is what Fanon (1967) refers to as an inherent narcissism of White racial superiority. All of this is further complicated by the cultural and racial disconnections, connections, matches, and mismatches that often emerge in classrooms between teachers and students (Milner, 2005).

Our journey does not lead to a minimizing of the lived experiences of the members of this classroom community, particularly for the benefit of classroom and teacher image management, but rather a maximization, building from and through experiences that are real. Doing so means that we are willing "to admit that to teach without biases requires that most of us learn anew, that we become students again" (hooks, 2010, p. 31); hence, the teacher is positioned outside of the expert role, which can be an uncomfortable experience for some.

Any exploration into Shoptalk as an instrument of teaching and learning must be ideologically and epistemologically open to accepting these mandates. As hooks (2010) reminds us, "Teachers must be open at all times, and we must be willing to acknowledge what we do not know" (p. 10). This acknowledgment requires a commitment to openness, honesty, and integrity by making explicit our areas of expertise *and* growth along with our students (hooks, 2010). When leveraged in the classroom, Shoptalk as community practice may provide an alternative space that structures opportunities for students to sort through the real-life dilemmas that they face, as well as work through the academic tasks they are expected to take up. When practiced in the classroom from the three orientations we discussed earlier (as a site of critical resistance), Shoptalk becomes part of a transformative, engaged approach to education and can provide robust learning opportunities that are simultaneously cultural, race conscious, and equity-oriented.

In the following chapter we will examine a new orientation—the *pedagogical orientation* of Shoptalk and the role of the instructor as cultural border crosser within that orientation. Through extended oral construction and deconstruction of one short but extremely provocative social text, we will see how students can not only gain required academic literacy skills but, equally important for students of color, actively collaborate and negotiate means of speaking back to disempowering texts.

CHAPTER 7

Shoptalk in the Classroom

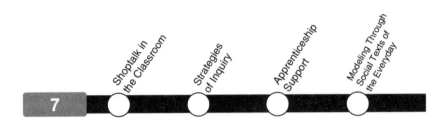

What does culturally responsive teaching and learning within problem-solving activities framed through Shoptalk look like within one urban language arts classroom?

Taking our seats we are now headed west, beyond the Magnificent Mile and across Chicago's West Side, where we will examine (1) how similar orientations and structures of participation with regard to the social reading of socially constructed narrative texts can occur in an language arts classroom; (2) how the performative aspects of Shoptalk contribute to individuals' reasoning about oral and written texts; and (3) how a group of African American high school students narrate their readings of culture, class, and other social relations in response to a social text that positions them in ways that compete with how they view themselves. As we take note of the shifting urban landscape surrounding the train, let me provide a cautionary road map to keep on hand as you consider the implications of teaching and learning from this perspective, perhaps in your own classroom.

There are a couple of assumptions, and some mandates that accompany these assumptions, with regard to where we are headed. First, our journey has not led us to "a destination of fabricated slaves and monsters" (Sartre, 2004, quoted in Leonardo & Porter, 2010, p. 140). Such a destination frames local knowledge and knowledge production on the part of the student as devalued and relegated to positions of subordination. This kind of minimization of student knowledge prevents learners from engaging in critical thinking where they might respond to or challenge the status quo (hooks, 2010). One might recall the political controversy in Texas and Arizona concerning a demand to eliminate classroom teaching that would develop critical thinking skills, in order to prevent students from challenging parental authority (Republican Platform Committee, 2012). However, silencing of student voices ignores the legacy of historical discrimination (Parker & Lynn, 2002) and students' capacity to think about, respond to, challenge, and shift perspectives about their experiences. Students not only should, but must, be encouraged and taught to think critically and question that which is impactful to their lives.

Rather, our travels lead us to a space where students must be viewed as critical thinkers who should be allowed to talk back in the instance where their lived experiences contribute to their capacity to learn and grow, especially when confronted with conditions of hegemony and racism they experience both inside and outside the classroom. According to Ladson-Billings and Donnor (2005), "Post-colonialism speaks to the collective project of the modern world that was in no way prepared for the decolonized [students that are the racialized 'Others'] to talk back and 'act up'" (p. 378). This act of "talking back" to the racial injustice and inequity that pervade their everyday lives suggests a conscious awareness and critical understanding of complex moral and ethical issues.

Second, the culmination of our journey should not be viewed as a reaffirmation of an already hostile and unsafe environment where too often students' perspectives and experiences are minimized. In the discourse on the national achievement gap, for example, student underperformance often is attributed to cultural deficits in parental education, income, and family structure. In Ruby Payne's *A Framework for Understanding Poverty* (2005), a cultural argument is presented as an explanation for the pervasive nature of the achievement gap, particularly between Black students and their White counterparts. However, according to critics of Payne's (2005) argument, such as Bomer et al. (2008) and Hughes and North (2012), as a consequence of focusing on the individual impediments to academic success in students' lives, "teachers may take away from Payne's work that it is adequate to focus on improving the 'deficient' knowledge and skills of poor students rather than the institutional factors that contributed to their life circumstances in the first place [and] such a focus too often precludes self-study by White and/or middle-class teachers about their own complicity in reproducing social inequities" (Hughes & North, 2012, p. 283). Rather, where we are headed is to a site, like the salon, of liberating possibilities and the disruption of violent truth claims regarding children and assumptive circumstances surrounding their lives, what hooks (2010) has called "biased dominator thinking" (p. 26), and what I call a racist savior habit of mind. This is not a site where teaching is akin to saving. Rather, it is a site where students come to recognize for themselves, as Darlene so aptly put it, "I wasn't scared of them, they were scared of me!"

SHOPTALK AS AN INSTRUCTIONAL MODEL

We are now within Shoptalk, where classroom teaching and learning are observed from three planes of analysis, *apprenticeship, guided participation*, and *participatory appropriation*. Drawing on the concepts of border crossing, counternarrative, social reading, dialogic argumentation, improvisation, and redirection that emerge from my observations of Shoptalk in the salon, I extended my consideration of Shoptalk to teaching and learning in formal environments, and the development of various designs of classroom instruction and curricular practices. In other words, Shoptalk is both cultural and institutional practice as well as a sensibility about these two things and a basis for inclusive and empowering classroom instruction. It propels student development through content-area practices that provide a space for cultural socialization within the discourse structure of the class. As an instructional tool, Shoptalk takes community-based practices that often are viewed as deficits, yet are akin to problem solving, and repositions these as robust sites of learning and development. Such practices foster interpretive skills, collaborative sensemaking and routine problem solving, personal and collective empowerment; provide opportunities for engagement in meaningful activities that are critical to cultural continuity; and teach young people the practice of using literate tools (such as improvisation, revision, irony, satire, contingency, narration, alternative possibilities, and unreliable narrator) to raise problems and explore possible worlds.

In an attempt to understand the role of talk and text in the learning that evolves within the classroom, my attention is drawn to locating, from each plane of analysis, the sources of support provided to students as they grapple with complex problem solving in the domain of response to literature. Additionally, I am concerned with the ways in which sociocultural activity is structured within the classroom, students' individual efforts to make sense of word and world, as well as the consequences of those efforts for changes in the quality of participation of students. A great deal can be learned about the ways in which each of these influences the learning of students who are presumed to be "at risk" and struggle in urban classrooms.

Contributing to this analysis are two underlying assumptions with regard to *pedagogical practices* and *curricular design*. First is the assumption that the classroom space *functions as a place of risk,* where students can collectively come to terms with the contradictions separating their own internally defined images of self as African American youth from the objectification as the Other (Hill-Collins, 2000). Based on the criteria for safe environments in schools and classrooms, outcome data clearly indicate that most urban schools serving largely low-income and minority students are neither physically nor intellectually and socially safe spaces. The enactment of a pedagogy of risk through Shoptalk involves a transformative approach to education, where, according to Banks (1998, 2001, 2003), the instructional aims are to teach students, as cultural border crossers, to think critically and to develop the skills to formulate, document, and justify their conclusions in domain-specific ways. It also involves a view of the world as socially constructed, narrative text and an awareness that through these texts people make sense of the world.

The second assumption is with regard to *curricular design*. The following sections explain key elements of the Shoptalk curriculum design and their incorporation of community discourse within the classroom. One very important design principle is that *classroom activity must be task directed*. This principle grounds itself in a particular disposition toward content knowledge. Key elements of this principle are derived from Lee's (2007) framework of Cultural Modeling.

Lee's framework of Cultural Modeling is subject-matter-task-specific and provides me with a set of analytical guidelines for the design of curriculum that, in part, draws upon the enactment of Shoptalk in the classroom. Of particular interest are the guidelines provided by Cultural Modeling for addressing how cultural funds of knowledge of students from diverse backgrounds align with the intellectual goals of academic subject-matter knowledge. These include the following:

- A careful task analysis of the kinds of problem-solving activities that are most generative within the subject matter
- A careful task analysis of the beliefs, language practices, and routine, everyday practices within the lives of a target body of students and the cognitive strategies demanded for participation in these practices
- Aligning the task analysis of the subject matter with that of the everyday practices
- Designing classroom activity and participation structures in which students metacognitively analyze their thinking in the everyday practices and over time are scaffolded to link those metacognitive analyses of their everyday thinking with their applications to subject-matter-specific tasks

Central to these guidelines is an acknowledgment of the fact that classroom activity does/should center around particular domain-specific tasks that both students and instructor confront through problem-solving activities.

Subject Matter as a Site of Apprenticeship

Within the Shoptalk classroom, the subject-matter focus[1] is on teaching students to respond to a variety of literature in ways that resemble how serious readers of canonical literature or literary critics respond.[2] By canonical literature, I am referring to a quality of literature that survives across time because of its presumed extraordinary attributes. Theorizing what an apprenticeship into the practices of response to literature calls for requires a reconceptualization of the secondary school's understanding of those demands. The traditional literature curriculum at the secondary school level is organized around genres, themes, and historical readings. Approaches to genre are often part of the first-year course focusing on the short story, the novel, poetry, and drama. It has been argued that these conceptions of genre are more descriptive and have little generative value for novices. For example, knowing the elements of the short story, such as rising action, denouement, and climax, as descriptors is insufficient to help a novice recognize the functions that each element serves in furthering the story. A primarily thematic approach can be useful in helping students make connections between the theme of a work and issues in their own lives. However, analyzing how a core set of themes is explored by different authors does not in itself help a struggling reader develop the tools for figuring out themes in multiple works on his or her own.

Finally, the historical organization of the literature curriculum in the traditional American and British literature courses places highly specialized demands on readers. In order to conduct a historical reading and construct sophisticated interpretations from this perspective, one must have a highly embedded understanding of the historical context of either the setting of the work, the time period in which the work was written, or the historical context of the author's personal and/or professional life. With these limitations in mind, it is especially problematic to apprentice such novice readers to learn or to want to engage in the practice of response to literature.

As an alternative, Lee (2007) makes the suggestion that we focus on what can be seen as more generative interpretive problems. Lee defines generativity in terms of the potential of strategies and habits of mind to help the novice tackle a wide array of problems in the subject matter. That is, generative interpretive problems have a potentially big bang for the buck. These generative interpretive problems include, but are not limited to, the following:

- Irony
- Satire
- Symbolism

- Use of unreliable narrators
- Structural ways of organizing literary texts such as stream of consciousness
- Typical patterns for representing character types, such as the picaresque hero

Lee recommends viewing the problems outlined as generative because one can use them in tackling problems in poetry, in drama, in short stories, in novels, and even in films. One can use them to tackle problems in 16th-century British poetry, in contemporary rap lyrics, or in what has come to be called word art.

In addition to a set of core interpretive problems, there are also the demands of habits of mind, ways of thinking about the uses of language, and the aesthetics of language use that characterize the discipline of response to literature. These include, but are not limited to, an appreciation for language play as an end in itself, not merely as a utilitarian tool of communication.

It is important to think of an apprenticeship as providing conceptual affordances. That is, in an apprenticeship one inherits a set of ways of thinking about a practice that generations before have found useful and productive. Participation in the practice also lends itself to extending the problem-solving tools across time. According to Hillocks (1982), "Involving students in using particular strategies of inquiry requisite to and underlying particular witting tasks is likely to result in greater gains than does involving them in the study of appropriate model" (p. 672). In this way, through participation, one inherits, appropriates, and expands the problem-solving tools available to the practice. So if one is learning to become a front-end associate in a hair salon, the novice does not have to invent ways of problem solving, but rather can take advantage of the strategies that are already available.

In the same sense, a novice reader does not have to construct tools for tackling a complex work of literature without any guidance. From this perspective, the constructs of and strategies for tackling problems of irony, for example, are conceptual tools for problem solving. They are in a sense inherited from the practice and extended by the practice. Each new generation of readers meets new expressions of irony. In making sense of these new representations of irony, new generations of readers both use inherited tools and adapt/construct new ones.

Apprenticeship into the practices of the community of readers of canonical literature also provides other kinds of inherited supports for problem solving. One set clearly includes the physical texts themselves: books, newspapers, magazines, the screen images of electronic texts, audio versions of books. A second set of supports includes activity structures like spoken word clubs, book clubs, online chat groups, author readings and lectures at bookstores, libraries, and schools/universities. Within such activity structures, novices and more knowledgeable others interact around their responses to works of literature. These activity structures become sites in which ways of reasoning about literature get passed on to others. And of course, there are the supports of school curriculum. There are also the interactions invited as novice and experienced readers read or hear critiques of literary works in the newspaper, journals, television, and radio. Thus, once one enters the stage of this ongoing drama involving literary readings, one walks into a set of ongoing practices and ways of thinking that support and influence how individuals come to be intense and strategic readers of canonical works of literature.

Strategies of Inquiry

According to Hillocks (2011), writing involves knowledge of both certain means of processing data (inquiry) and discourse knowledge. Students must learn both strategies of inquiry and those of instantiating certain kinds of writing. Writers need two kinds of knowledge: strategies for inquiring into the substance of writing and strategies for producing various kinds of discourse. In order to write an original text, writers first must conduct an inquiry into the data at hand. Such an inquiry is guided by a set of heuristics —procedures for discovering the propositions that the arguments are intended to support. The purpose of such heuristic procedures is to ensure that their users make systematic and thorough examinations of any subject approached for writing. While heuristics are powerful in providing guidelines for the systematic analysis of data, they tend to subsume at each level of abstraction a variety of skills and strategies that appear to be fundamental to their effective use, but are often complex in and of themselves.

Therefore, Hillocks suggests the use of what he calls *strategies of inquiry* (1982), consciously adopted procedures used to investigate phenomena in various unrelated disciplines for the purpose of producing insights.

> Strategies of inquiry include observing, describing, and comparing/contrasting. They lead to and are necessary to generalizations of three increasingly complex types (enumerative, definitory, and hypothetical), each of which must be examined with varying degrees of experimental rigor (depending the discipline) through further observation description, and comparison/contrast to determine reliability and validity. Further, it is clear that observation is basic to the description of particular instances, that the description (or recognition of details)

permits the comparison and or contrast of instances, and that the latter is the basis for enumerative generalizations. (pp. 665–666)

The cornerstone of inquiry as a means of processing data is the idea of a thesis, or question and potential evidence that bears on it. Entertaining a thesis that is understood as capable of being disconfirmed by evidence sets the stage for the coordination of theory and evidence that lies at the heart of inquiry. Our goal in instruction is to provide structured supports to students' inquiry efforts, in particular by scaffolding the process of question generation and, throughout the activity, prompting students to identify what their procedures indicate with respect to the question. Ultimately, what we would like students to do is present an argument in which data are used to justify claims, and to present and link data to conclusions. As they engage in inquiry, students are constructing mental models of the phenomena they examine and also developing their own more general mental model of how causes and effects operate. The assumption here is that, just as with the women in the salon, students have formulated theories as a means of understanding the world.

Apprenticeship Support in the Shoptalk Classroom

The hair salon provided us with a glimpse into the habits of mind of the women and men in the salon, and the kinds of social, and arguably academic, practices that can occur in African American community settings, practices that contribute to learning. Earlier chapters of this book focused on talk as a kind of public performance and discourse, where patrons and workers play out scripted roles as social actors who effortlessly and deliberately take center stage.

These readings and the skills associated with them are not unlike those taken up in most language arts classrooms and center around the kinds of social and cultural border crossing that happens across the life span as people negotiate a range of cross-cultural encounters. Our concern in the Shoptalk classroom is to teach students to respond to texts in ways that resemble what serious, expert readers of social texts (inside and outside the salon) do. These include the following:

- Recognize the elements of the story, including narrative
- Understand the purposes of personal narrative in relation to the theme
- Make predictions with regard to the results of the text and counter-text

- Understand the context of the text as situated and adapt to shifts derived from meanings embedded in that context
- Recognize emotional and ideological overtones in the text and their relationship to outcomes of the text
- Recognize the historical situatedness of the fuller text
- Recognize the role of AAE in the production of text

Navigating such readings, therefore, places particular internal (at times emotional) demands of the interpretive problem on the participants if they are to construct sophisticated interpretations of the text. An awareness of and appreciation for such social, oral texts can be useful in helping students make connections between some particular issue within the text and issues in their own lives. However, analyzing how an issue is explored by an author (or group of folks in a salon) does not in and of itself help a novice develop tools for figuring out the issue in multiple works on her own.

The skills involved in the reading of social texts are culturally situated literate skills used for crossing borders of culture, class, and language. These skills include, but are not limited to, awareness of norms and rhetorical structures, inferencing, improvisation, and signification. In addition to the affordances of the practices within subject matter, I draw on the affordances of the everyday practices of students, what they inherit from their lived experiences in the world. This is in alignment with both Shoptalk and the Cultural Modeling design for classroom instruction. After careful task analysis of the generative problems in the subject matter, I look to the structure and subject matter of the routine, everyday practices of Shoptalk that align directly or indirectly with the target academic tasks.

Two apprenticeship models are useful here: learning to tackle interpretive problems in canonical literature and learning to tackle interpretive problems in the discourse of Shoptalk in and out of the classroom. In both, people inherit from their participation certain ways of reasoning, certain tools and artifacts (both physical and conceptual), certain routinized activities, and certain social relationships that together support and extend mental functioning. Conceptually, each apprenticeship model provides designers of curriculum and learning environments affordances to support student learning. From a design perspective, such task analysis and alignment open opportunities for teachers and curriculum specialists to take seriously the prior knowledge of students of color, students whose first language is other than English, and students living in low-income communities.

MODELING THROUGH TEXTS OF THE EVERYDAY

A central tenet of the Shoptalk curriculum (derived from Cultural Modeling) is to begin instruction with modeling activities that draw on students' prior knowledge. Modeling is a process by which the teacher makes public to students those strategies and habits of mind that the students are expected to eventually be able to carry out on their own. In reciprocal teaching, for example, the teacher stands before the class and asks questions, makes predictions, and clarifies uncertainties about a text the teacher and students are reading jointly. Through such activities, the teacher models what the students will be asked to carry out as instruction progresses. In my classroom, modeling begins with something similar to what Lee (2007) calls cultural data sets. Cultural data sets are texts—print, music, video, art—with which we presume students are already very familiar because they engage with these texts in their home and community, as part of their everyday practices. These everyday cultural texts place interpretive demands similar to those the students will meet in the canonical texts that follow in the instructional sequence.

The purpose for the use of such culturally familiar texts is that they:

- Provide students with support for making public and explicit the tacit knowledge they possess about how to make sense of a particular kind of problem
- Provide students with a language to talk about their problem-solving processes; help students make connections between what they already do and what they are expected to do with canonical, school-based problems
- Establish a culture of inquiry, or argumentation with evidence, of hypothesizing, and of intellectual risk taking as norms for participation in class
- Socialize students into using particular habits of mind that are specific to the discipline in question, and the particular ways that inquiry, argumentation with evidence, hypothesizing, and risk taking are characteristic of responses to literature, mathematics, history, or science

Lee offers as examples of cultural data sets R&B rap lyrics, rap videos, stretches of signifying dialogues (a genre of talk in AAE), as well as film clips and television programs. Building on Lee's suggestion, modeling texts within the Shoptalk curriculum, or texts of the everyday, must meet some additional requirements:

- They must speak to a particular issue or problem of genuine concern to the lives of the students as members of the community.
- The issue must be rooted in a conflict between an institutional perspective and values and lived cultural perspectives and values.
- They must create a rupture between reader expectation and reader experience.
- They must represent a veiled argument of fact that in and of itself is a claim.
- They must invite a process of inquiry through which it becomes necessary to identify veiled parts of the full argument.
- They must position lived experiences of the readers in opposition to the claims made by the institutional point of view.
- They must prompt the reader to problem-solve by generating an understanding of the claim set forth by the text through inferencing.

In the Shoptalk classroom, students first are provided with a text of the everyday. Embedded within that text is a claim or statement representing a veiled argument of fact. Within the classroom, students engage in the process of social reading, unpacking the text in which they, as African American adolescents, are positioned in a particular way by the author. The activity of unpacking the text is an instance of social reading that facilitates the instructional goal, which in the unit I describe here was that by the end of the unit (introducing students to canonical structures of argumentation), students should have a better understanding of the nature of argument and the routine strategies that are involved in justifying claims and generating counterclaims.

With that objective, students were asked to consider the following text of the claim made by former U.S. secretary of education (1983–1988) William Bennett, in which he publicly stated the following on his radio show, *Morning in America*, on September 28, 2005:

> If you wanted to reduce crime, you could—if that were your sole purpose—you could abort every Black baby in this country and your crime rate would go down. That would be an impossibly ridiculous and morally reprehensible thing to do, but your crime rate would go down.

At the time it was made, Bennett's comment ignited a firestorm of discussion throughout the media (and hair salons and barbershops, I'm sure). Much of the discussion centered on the appropriateness and/or inappropriateness of the statement, which was made within a broader discussion around the idea of social safety within the United States. Bennett's remark is disturbing, to say the least. However, situated within Shoptalk, it became useful as a target of social reading. In the Shoptalk classroom, the selection of texts and writing activities is intended to help students interrogate the word and the world. It also is intended to mediate the larger task of grappling with a complex text as an instance of argument. These texts of the everyday ask students to engage with issues within their own lives and in a broader social context, generating a critical understanding of the issues at hand, as well as the skills required to grapple with one's emotional reactions, understand alternative perspectives, and generate counterarguments. The actions required to generate a counterargument, or speak back to disempowering texts, are akin to those taken up by cultural border crossers each day.

First, this text mirrored the kinds of events or texts that get taken up in the hair salon and whose features I characterized above. Second, it reflected the ideas, values, beliefs, attitudes, languages, and dispositions of a socially contingent discourse and discourse community. Third, in addition to an awareness of its discourse features, there are the taken-for-granted knowledge, skills, and behaviors necessary for membership in the discourse community of that purely statistically oriented text-world. Fourth, such a text-world functions as borders, where movement across can be difficult as it relies on knowledge, skill, and a way of behaving that may not be readily available or valuable to the student as a member of the African American community. Such features within (and external to) the text revealed themselves as being useful in facilitating an alignment with the kinds of practices that get performed in the salon *and* the intellectual goals of academic subject-matter knowledge of understanding argumentation.

For example, the structure of Bennett's claim reflects a veiled argument of which only part, the claim, is immediately available, while the other attributes (grounds, backing, warrants, or rules that provide generally accepted reasoning for a claim) are taken for granted as they do not appear within the actual text. Any reader of this claim must make certain assumptions and draw on particular prior knowledge or rules in order to make sense of the claim. Often these rules are a part of the taken-for-granted knowledge of the individual, as is the case here.

What is most interesting about this claim, particularly with regard to Shoptalk, is that the veiled argument stated by Bennett as a claim itself positions the reader in certain ways (regardless of background) and requires some unpacking, a process that reveals its hidden parts. In other words, as a reader you must make certain choices with regard to what you understand to be the warrants to the claim in order to make sense of it. In this case, and in order to see this as a claim, the accepted rule would have to be that crime statistics broken out by ethnicity are an acceptable value-free basis for offering a theoretical, although "reprehensible," solution.

In this case, that solution embodies acceptance of two racist and horrific assumptions: that Black babies are not only extinguishable but that there is a benefit to this. It is the very nature of the warrants that provide the grounds for the claim and that distinguish the reader, depending on how close he or she is to the situation. It is also the very nature of the warrants that make it useful within the Shoptalk view of cultural data set. In other words, Bennett's remarks are a claim outside of any clear and stated evidence to support it, but the claim also can be an argument when you look at certain taken-for-granted assumptions or knowledge that the author is trying to set forth.

As part of the task, students have to look at this as a claim and locate the taken-for-granted beliefs, assumptions, and rules that the author draws from and that make this an accepted or unaccepted argument. It is a process that can be articulated to students as following the author's line of reasoning, "a train of reasoning," to try to determine how he arrived at his conclusion. Chapter 8 shows how students and I took up this task, following its line of reasoning, as an instance of text examination and problem solving within Shoptalk.

Students use strategies of inquiry to critically examine issues both inside and outside the classroom in order to attend to a situated dilemma presented as a claim within the Bennett text. Engagement here is a social and cultural, as well as a literacy, event, with critical engagement, ideological stances, and counternarratives enacted in the classroom—a space that has social, political, ideological, historical, cultural, and literate dimensions.

INQUIRY INTO TEXTS OF THE EVERYDAY

One of the most challenging pedagogical principles that Lee's Cultural Modeling framework extends to any classroom instructor is grounded in the idea of negotiating *metacognitive instructional conversations* around cultural data sets (Lee, 2007). Metacognition refers to people's abilities to monitor (think about) their current level of thinking or understanding and decide when it is not adequate (Bransford, Brown, & Cocking, 2000). In other words, thinking about thinking. In these metacognitive instructional conversations, the teacher supports students in articulating how it is that they know what they know. Often this knowledge is based on some existent set of data. Within Shoptalk discourse, that data source was often in the form of some original source (e.g., the Bible, historical document, personal correspondence, legal record, and so forth) in addition to a narrative account (e.g., "When my son was having trouble with math, I used an egg timer to help him out"). This is critically important here, because one of the instructional goals within this unit on argumentation was to guide students in their understanding of William Bennett's claim, which must be assumed to stand on certain merits that have to be identified.

Students need little help in recognizing that, as former secretary of education, Bennett sits in a position of public authority. It would be easy for anyone to trust his statements based solely on his social/political standing given that he served as President Reagan's chairman of the National Endowment for the Humanities (1981–1985) and secretary of education (1985–1988), later as President Bush's "drug czar" (1989–1990), and now as host of his nationally syndicated radio show *Bill Bennett's Morning in America* and author of numerous best-selling books (including *The Book of Virtues for Young People: A Treasury of Great Moral Stories*).

Such authority often is mistaken as sufficient in warranting any assertion made by the individual. This is akin to the notion that "if it's in the book, it must be true" (Hillocks, 2011, p. 68). Regardless of the inhumanity of this particular suggestion, under these circumstances students (and many adults) may avoid any critical thinking, abdicating any responsibility to go back to the text.

This is a critical turning point in literacy engagement where Shoptalk, as a pedagogical and problem-solving tool, can be most useful.

In framing talk in a particular way within the classroom, Shoptalk gives students the help they need to publicly (1) challenge and/or support the assertion; (2) articulate how they know this assertion is with or without grounds; and (3) locate the particular grounds that an author may or may not use to support that claim or assertion.

From such conversations, students begin to construct a set of heuristics that they then can explicitly draw on as they do the work of locating the problem within the text, and from this experience learning to interrogate other texts. In doing so, students must actively think about their thinking, while engaging with data and their implications. Constructing or evaluating an argument for or against someone else's claim requires identifying the other's perspective and coordinating it with other elements. As they engage in such inquiry using the questions below, students are more likely to construct an explicit mental model or script for explicating and responding to this and other texts and arguments.

- What is the speaker saying and what are the assumptions (personal beliefs) behind what the speaker is saying?
- What is the speaker inferring and on what are these inferences based?
- What are the broader issues surrounding the statement being made and are they well presented and supported?

- How is the discussion being framed? Who's speaking on it and setting up how it is being talked about?
- What is being omitted?
- What interpretations and hypotheses are being made?
- What questions guide our interpretations?
- What do we already know?
- How does what we know compare with these new data?
- What possibilities are being thrown out?

In the service of domain-specific reasoning, Shoptalk does several important things. First, Shoptalk provides structured supports and a space where learners can develop these skills. Much like performing athletes, those socialized into Shoptalk develop a disposition toward problem solving in that they learn to recognize that they must be able to read the floor, run plays, and predict opponents' actions (Nasir, 2011). This process, in its own right, is culturally meaningful and rife with powerful opportunities for youth of varying ability levels to participate and develop their skills while interacting with one another. Everyone is a teacher and a learner simultaneously; everyone has the ability, with hard work, to be a player (Gomez & Pinkard, 2014).

Additionally, Shoptalk scaffolds the process of question generation and response at various levels of abstraction through which students' inquiry efforts are aimed. In this case, students are addressing particular problems of both world and word—in other words, locating and addressing Bennett's assertion. In fact, in this instance of classroom activity, there are two overarching problems for the students to solve regarding the above assertion, both tied to the overall goal of understanding the nature of arguments people offer to support their theories. The first problem is: How does Bennett set about producing an argument in defense of his claim? In other words, *what gets read by Bennett and is it sufficient to support the claim that he is making?*

The second problem regards the problem-solving strategies themselves: What modes of criticism and assessment are appropriate to consider when assessing the merits of the argument that Bennett presents? In other words, *who gets to be the reader and what tools or skills are they able to apply?* Shoptalk provides (1) tools through which participants can not only address the problem, but collectively come to terms with the contradictions separating their own internally defined images of self as African American youth from objectification as the Other (Hill-Collins, 2000), and (2) a structured space where students grapple with how knowledge is produced, consumed, and reproduced for future use. As in the hair salon, students' engagement with this and similar texts can be viewed as a shared, dialogic process of understanding and making public to an audience how they think—particularly with regard to problems posed within texts—how they access an author's thinking, and how that thinking shapes present and future actions. And in the case of a hurtful text such as Bennett's, students can engage with it within a supportive social classroom community.

As discussed more fully in Chapter 2, in dialogic argumentation, one must recognize an opposition between two assertions (in this case, Bennett's assertion and the community's). Evidence then must be related to each of the assertions, and if the argument is to move toward resolution, this evidence needs to be weighed through an integrative group evaluation of the relative merits of the opposing assertions. As was seen in our earlier illustration of the women in the salon debating the merits of one young mother's decision to send her child to live with the child's father, adult participants of Shoptalk use both their individual and collective readings of social texts to challenge the *content and the form of reasoning process* of the young mother. In this context, both the readings of events (framed by the claim posited by the adolescent, and the counter-readings offered by the adults) function as tools for socializing the young women into alternative readings and hence alternative points of view of that text.

Competent argumentative reasoning requires the ability to reflect on one's own thinking as an object of thought. "In the absence of this ability one's beliefs are utilized as the basis for organizing and interpreting experience, but only by means of this second order, reflective thinking ability can one think about, evaluate, and hence be in a position to justify these beliefs (Kuhn, 1991, p. 14). When viewed this way, Shoptalk offers us a way to externalize the internal thinking strategies that youth engage in and that many classroom teachers would like to foster with their students. As Kuhn asserts, "This externalization serves not only the research objective of analysis, but also the practical objective of facilitation" (p. 23). The discussion in Chapter 8 of classroom activity surrounding Bennett's claim yielded several stories, four of which I share. Each story speaks to the intersection of Shoptalk and literacy learning at the plane of guided participation.

The Classroom as a Site of Guided Participation

How do community-based discourse norms, structures, and content of argumentation (similar to those located in the hair salon) provide participation structures that invite engagement with complex problem solving?

The sociolinguistic literature confirms that speakers of AAE participate in speech and discourse genres in which indirection and frequent use of figurative language abounds. Like the men and women in the salon, however, students' abilities to interpret literary tropes embedded in the context of their everyday language was tacit.

CURRICULUM DESIGN

In the Shoptalk classroom, units of instruction are organized around interpretive problems and draw upon the Cultural Modeling design principles described earlier. This 3-week instructional unit focused on argumentation, with the goal of helping students acquire an understanding of the nature of argument and the routine strategies that are involved in justifying claims and generating counterclaims. In addition, the goal was for students to construct representations of arguments and counterarguments, with special attention to the use of grounds and warrants that required complex inferencing and use of metaphor. Explicitly, we wanted students to engage in those critical thinking practices that are applied by better readers in general, but specifically readers of social text. These include asking questions, making predictions, monitoring one's understanding while reading, adjusting one's predictions based on new textual evidence, making connections across sentences and paragraphs, and using one's prior knowledge to help understand the text.

Although the Common Core Standards speak to the need to prepare students for future situations where the skills of argument would be useful, they present a view that, while inclusive of certain kinds of readings, omits consideration of *how similar ideas and value systems operate in other kinds of readings and the skills involved in critiquing them.*

STORY ONE: EMBODYING THE JALI

Drawing from experiences in the salons with regard to developing an understanding of community norms for talk in teaching and learning, I look to African American English (AAE), a legitimate and systematic language variety of English often demonized within the United States, as a positive, institutional resource that my African American students and I share.

The use of the Bennett text allows me to model for students what reasoning looks like, providing a culturally situated problem whose solutions mirror the academic task I want the students to learn—how to identify and construct a reasoned argument. At this point, the assumption is that students have not been exposed to the text outside of class and are unfamiliar with both Bennett and his comment. Nor have they been exposed to the text as a cultural data set within this or any other unit of instruction. The plan for this instructional unit was to look deeply and in multiple ways at this very short but provocative piece of text. Following my introduction of the text, students would gain practice and facility in all of the following tools of inquiry, metacognition, analysis, talking back to text, and representation of ideas:

- Conversation in large and small groups
- Journaling
- Construction of counterarguments
- Debate
- Letter writing

Shoptalk served as a pedagogical tool, with its structure and norms in the service of instruction and maintenance of a safe space. I positioned myself as a cultural border crosser, in that I am both teacher and African American community member. I make the distinction between my participation and positioning in the two communities, characterizing Bennett as "this man on the radio." This positioning, established through rhetorical structures and features of AAE, places the instructor as social actor in the role of social reader, in which she revoices what can be considered the official point of view of the radio show. I accomplish this much the same way as Ms. Addie does, by setting up the characters of the event, stressing racial distinctions ("Bennett"), changing volume and intonation when adding the qualifier, "a White man."

> *Instructor:* Today we gone talk about something that, the more I think about it, the more it doesn't make any sense to me.
> *Student:* What we gone talk about today? I thought we was startin' argument?
> *Instructor:* We are, and that's exactly what I'm talkin' about. This White man on the radio said . . .

Here, my intonation rises sharply. However, when I say, "Black babies," in contrast to my reference to Bennett as a White man, I slow down in my speech for emphasis when I get to the crucial point in the claim, which is, "you could abort every Black baby . . . and your crime rate would go down." This reading is spaced out, lending to dramatic ironic effect. My aim was to establish ironic tension, something the performers of Shoptalk displayed in the salon. Such dramatic effect, through linguistic and paralinguistic features, is a part of what defines the African American hair salon and classroom as AAE speech communities.

Students are cooperating with respect to the dramatic tension. The jointly shared responses of the students, with spontaneous, exaggerated eye gestures and verbal responses, indicate their engagement and signal the gravity of Bennett's assertion as well as their mutual understanding as to the motives of their instructor's linguistic act, and the duality of my role as border crosser. The exchange, therefore, is produced jointly by an active audience, who by virtue of its participation brings a shared knowledge of the norms of AAE, one that goes beyond the traditional classroom participation structure of I-R-E (Initiate, Respond, Evaluate), to bear on its constructions.

While reading the racialized subtext of Bennett's claim, I also am reading the responses of my students and acknowledging their positionings through that reading. Racially charged messages embedded in a text like that of Bennett can be considered offensive and harmful. However, it is important to remember what hooks (2010) describes as "learning past the hate." In her essay of the same title, she states that "more than ever before, students need to learn from unbiased perspectives, be they conservative or radical [and] more than ever before, students and teachers need to fully understand differences of nationality, race, sex, class and sexuality if we are to create ways of knowing that reinforce education as the practice of freedom" (p. 110). It is here that the notion of a critical reading of text is illuminated as participants' prior understandings of the phenomenon (White enactment of power), and resistance to that phenomenon (wary responses), take center stage and get taken up.

When Ms. Addie relates her experiences, her narrative is represented to an audience that shares a core set of experiences and linguistic norms. Similarly, as instructor, my reading of Bennett is represented to an audience that also shares such norms. One could argue that Ms. Addie sees herself as culture worker, serving in the tradition of Jali or Griot, as one who interprets the word and world and seeks the psychological, cultural, and physical liberation of Black people on all levels. As instructor, I take my cue from this positioning, as many instructors before me have done; my reading of the event is structured by an African American narrative style in which I direct the speech encounter, with the audience participating minimally.

STORY TWO: INTRODUCING THE PROBLEM

Group problem solving in the hair salon was viewed as a situated event where the *process of coming to know* was considered equally as important as the conclusions drawn. The structure of Darlene's narrative of her encounter with a group of White men while vacationing contributed to a dialogic group dynamic within the salon. This narrative structure was absolutely critical, with regard not just to the group but to the nature of development and meaning-making through guided participation in this context. This is apparent, as the narrative and the group contributions to its construction provided insights into the individual participants' readings of the social and cross-cultural relations that may not have been apparent in the actual encounter. Positioning here is important, as it illuminates a critical issue in this idea of *reading the Other*. That is, skills of social readings are likely to be displayed only in context-appropriate ways. The example of Ms. Addie also illustrates how such readings may be performed most dramatically and openly in situations in which the author/speaker feels confident that her audience will share her reading.

I drew from my awareness of participants' positioning within the process of problem solving in the salon to guide students' development and problem solving with regard to Bennett. Attentive to the norms of Shoptalk, like AAE, I employed an additional feature of the community-based, problem-solving discourse: a separation of self from text. The events and practices around grappling with the Bennett question can be taken as the actions through which critical engagement, ideological stances, and counter-narratives are enacted in the classroom, a space that has social, political, ideological, historical, cultural, and literate dimensions. Shoptalk contributed to the nature of classroom discourse, as here we returned to the creation of liberatory safe space—that is, a class where participants can talk about/write about what is meaningful to their lived lives.

Understanding and Separation of Self from Themes Within the Text

In introducing the problem of Bennett's argument, I recognized that it was going to be necessary for students to face the contradictions faced by many other African Americans around self and socially defined images, and to call forth the processes for grappling with these. While the instructional goal was to teach students to identify how authors might construct arguments concerning everyday matters that go beyond traditional text models, ultimately and collectively the process for getting there called for making explicit how others think, what constitutes the subject of thought, and how to respond in future action. As in the hair salon, this process involved a coming to terms with the contradictions inherent in Bennett's assertion—a separating of one's own thinking and self from that of others. Following my introduction of the text, I asked students to take a few moments and document in their journals their initial thoughts about the claim. While I was keenly aware that there were certain things I could assume my students were able to do or were aware of, it is also important to note that I recognized that there were things that they may not have been able to do or needed to be made aware of.

For example, I knew that it was important to not take for granted that many adolescent students often lack the fuller awareness of racial issues, such as those understood by older adults. At the very least, their level of awareness was not going to be as high or as clear as one might expect. This was evident to me in the class as our engagement with the Bennett text transitioned beyond students' initial reactions to the identification and analysis of the argument and problem within the text. My assumption was that students had experienced some level of racial socialization within their home and community environments. However, it was not my expectation that students initially would know that they were not born with racial awareness or knowledge of differences instantiated in racialized identities, but rather were taught it. While many students expressed shock and indicated both orally and in written form that they did not agree with or were bothered by the text, they didn't seem to make a connection between their beliefs and where their beliefs came from. Seldom, when asked to identify the origins of their own beliefs with regard to race, class, and gender, did students respond confidently.

Responses Situated Around Comprehension of Texts

There are two levels of problem here. First, the literal level: Students could not get the basic intention of the text. Second, the critical level: Students did not analyze ideas in the text critically, making connections between the text and their knowledge of world. Nor did they draw causal relationships between the text and root causes. They did not question or challenge the text beyond objecting to it and finding it disturbing.

The following are examples of students' written responses.

Example One:
"This passage is appalling. How could someone be so selfish? The comment that this man says is very ignorant. He is saying that our ethnic background is the main reason why the crime rate is so high."

Example Two:
"I feel that this man was wrong and that the comment was full of bigotry. He should be ashamed of himself and offer his apology to all African Americans."

Example Three:
"The comments made by Bennett are clearly the result of an ignorant mind reluctant to release his prejudices and misconceptions on another."

Example Four:
"I believe that Bennett is terribly ignorant and insensitive. Bennett's remarks are very hurtful and helps my belief that there is still racism in the world."

Students' expressions of feeling are a good thing here, in that they make students' thinking public and reveal that students see themselves within the text and are aware that the author has made certain choices here, choices with which the students can choose to agree or disagree. Students' displays of anger in the above passages should be interpreted positively. According to Leonardo and Porter (2010), too often Whites interpret minority anger as a distancing move, or the confirmation of the "angry" person of color archetype, rather than its opposite: an attempt to engage the Other to be vulnerable to the Other, to be recognized by the Other, to be the Other for the Other. As Freire (1993) once remarked, protestation from the oppressed is an act of love insofar as it represents an act of engagement. When the oppressed open their wounds through communication, they express the violence in their dehumanization that they want the oppressor to recognize. People of color fear not only overt violence from Whites (although this would be enough), but rather their wantonness, their lack of recognition of people of color—a certain violence of the heart rather than the fist.

This is what Fanon (2004) describes as "violence rippling under the skin" (p. 31). This secondary form of violence confirms a daily assault that often goes unnoticed. It is a double violence that fails to acknowledge the Other on whom one imposes an unwelcome will (Leonardo & Porter, 2010). Hence, by displaying their feelings as an initial reaction in response to Bennett, students are engaging with the text, bringing to the fore that something is wrong with this assertion. They are aware of something being wrong and are curious as to the point of the author's claim.

In each of the above examples, the student expresses horror in addition to making judgments about Bennett's character. However, none appears to address the argument Bennett is making. The traditional participation structure of I-R-E (Initiate, Respond, Evaluate) is one in which the teacher, in initiating the text, will evaluate students' responses as either appropriate or inappropriate. In this structure, the process ends with the evaluation, where the students take away from it the *correct*, yet uninterrogated and unapplied answer. However, it is in the aftermath of the initial response to the text where instruction can move beyond the traditional structure, into a deeper engagement that is safe space, where I-R-E is transformed to I-R-A (initiate, respond, apply). In this format, the student, after making the initial response, is pushed to justify the response and to re-evaluate it against the text. In addition, participation is not teacher directed but rather student driven.

In example four, the student appears to find Bennett's comment symptomatic of society's racism. As a result, there is an interaction here between audience and speaker, undergirded by a self-awareness of belief systems and values. Through shared understandings, students were able to see how statements or text by default positions them as readers, and, as in this case, subjects of this text. They are able to see how power operates through language, specifically how they are labeled and represented to a larger audience. However, through the process of socially working through the text, and their readings of it, students were able to reposition themselves in relation to that text and to reposition how they responded to it in socially and academically productive ways. This structure allowed students to enact roles within the participation structure, as opposed to being positioned within them, with narrative telling acting as a literacy tool that in turn helped them cope with this act of being forcefully and succinctly positioned by one glib statement.

Finally, in secondary language arts classrooms, students must learn to grapple with complex ideas and values that may exclude or demean their cultural backgrounds and experiences embedded in literary texts. As instructors, we must realize and accept that for many students of color, attacks on their personhood occur when there is an absence of recognition of the embedded attacks (the silences) and not just when they are made explicit as in the Bennett piece.

Spaces of learning must be created in which students can identify and navigate the problem-solving tasks that lie at the intersection of their own lives and the academic task of understanding complex literary text. As a liberatory safe space, this classroom is a site of culture, negotiation, and constructed knowledge where students initially were allowed emotional and visceral responses to a text that they deemed threatening to their lives and insulting to their experiences.

Just as Darlene's restatement of her story, "I wasn't scared of them, they were scared of me," summarized the narrative without making explicit who is supposed to be scared of whom or even why one has to be scared of the other, such restatement directs the audience's thinking to interpret the unstated instructional meanings of the narrated event centering on the issue of racial conflict. The fact that the students were provided opportunity, with cultural supports, to openly grapple with the veiled assumptions and causal assertions of Bennett's claim, made it more likely that they would raise their own questions moving forward and challenge the thinking of Bennett, the teacher, and one another. Thus, from the very first day of the modeling activity, this particular cultural data set helped establish boundaries about who could talk, about what, when, and how.

Viewing literacy as grounded in one's ways of being in the world situates students as contributors to the learning process and acknowledges students' cultural practices. A cultural view of literacy (grounded in students' ways of listening, speaking, and responding) can inform the creation of learning environments in which teachers and students collaborate to access and solve problems in literary texts through the ways in which they learn in their everyday lives as community members. Acknowledging these practices as resources for learning allows for a student-centered, culturally responsive approach to literacy instruction. Such an approach provides an opportunity for learners to make use of familiar and unfamiliar ideas and values in meaningful ways, in which students demonstrate literacy skills.

STORY THREE: NARRATIVE IMPROVISATION AS A PEDAGOGICAL TOOL

"One of the critical skills of Jali is her/his ability to improvise."
—Ralph Ellison, 1999

Improvisation refers to the expert art of jazz musicians "performing spontaneously, without the aid of manuscript, sketches or memory." Such definitions, suggests Berliner (1994), "reflect the common view that the activity of improvisation comprises neither the faithful recreation of a composition nor the elaboration of prefigured ideas" (pp. 1–2). Berliner continues:

> When players use improvisation as a noun, referring to improvisations as artistic products, they typically focus on the products' precise relationship to the original models that inspired them. . . . When artists use improvise as a verb, however, they focus not only on the degree to which old models are transformed and new ideas created, but on the dynamic conditions and precise processes underlying their transformation and creation. (p. 221)

Ellison harnesses the verb here, and draws our attention to the part and to the whole, the old and the new. While playing together, each musician is in a successive solo where he or she is competing with the others for space. Such competition takes place within a larger production, within which the individual contribution makes the whole piece better.

In employing the Shoptalk discourse within large- and small-group work, students were able to view and to use discursive practices familiar to them and similar to those identified within the Shoptalk discourse. Characteristic features of AAE discourse, including multiparty-overlapping talk, call and response, narrative sequencing, and verbal inventiveness, similarly mark talk in this class, like that of the hair salon. Lee (2007) characterizes instructional talk based on African American English norms as improvisation:

> It is improvisational because how it emerges and flows cannot be predicted in advance. . . . It operates very much like jazz where the band begins with a joint melody that follows a riff that is both responsive to what all the other players are doing, but is also unique; a kind of call and response conversation among musical interlocutors. . . . Such instructional improvisations are hybrid in nature . . . because they involve an interweaving, in this case of African American English Vernacular discourse patterns and canonical literary reasoning. The teacher then must understand where is the literary reasoning in the AAEV discourse and how is the AAEV discourse structured. (p. 96)

It is the teacher's job to manage such improvisations "because the teacher, as the representative of the domain knowledge into which students are being apprenticed, must understand what students' statements signify about their emerging understanding; not just their understanding of the text or specific problem being discussed, but rather of how what they say about the text problem reveals something about their more general knowledge of the discipline" (Lee, 2007, p. 95). Just as each musician recognizes that there is a shift in play as the musicians move between contexts of self and whole, so too must the instructor recognize such shifts in the occasion of student reasoning.

In the classroom, I found it useful to model this process through *the kinds of narrative retelling* that we saw in the hair salons. For example, as part of this unit students were assigned to opposing debate teams, one rejecting Bennett's claim, the other supporting it. During preparation for the debate, I stood next to the table of students who were to oppose Bennett, the "law firm representing Black kids that get to be born." I looked at them and said, "This is serious." The expressions on their faces reflected an understanding of the seriousness of this issue. Employing this law role-play afforded students on the opposing side of the debate the opportunity to come to terms with the contradictions involved in separating their feelings and thinking about Bennett's comments from those of the lawyers in this law firm. It afforded them the opportunity to engage without invalidating the feelings they had about a potentially offensive claim.

The signifying that took place here drew on a pedagogical toolkit familiar to members of the community. Signifying, which involves using metaphor as illustrations or explanations, is a culturally situated tool in the African American community and, as such, allowed students to grapple with their reactions to Bennett's claim through a culturally bound teaching strategy while simultaneously taking up an alternative perspective (i.e., that of the law firm or Bennett) without their own feelings entering their critiques. Narrative retelling, therefore, becomes an aspect of the guided participation that occurred within the classroom. By providing ongoing, synchronous feedback on student responses in terms of how they added to or constrained the evolving argument, we invoked tools of Shoptalk in students' attempts to come to know.

STORY FOUR: CRITICAL ACTION AND REASONING

In enacting a liberatory safe space, we can view this classroom as a site of culture, negotiation, and constructed knowledge where students initially were allowed emotional and visceral responses to a text that they deemed threatening to their lives and insulting to their experiences. This event speaks to what goes on in many mainstream classrooms where students are asked to respond to a text. What is often absent from this process of engaging readers is a pushback, or rather a space where perspectives can be interrogated through cultural meanings and norms.

Following the journal assignment, I revisited and specified the routine strategies and skills it takes to identify claims within traditional structures of argument, the kind framing Bennett's claim, by reading the various texts surrounding it and taking an inquiry approach to problem solving. Such reading also involved students' active evaluation of Bennett (as protagonist), whose actions, thoughts, and feelings were interpreted in light of local notions of what is right and wrong, just and unjust. In taking this approach, students confronted their derived understanding of the meaning in Bennett's statement and held it as a claim that, in order to be a true argument, must have certain warrants that could establish it as truth. This meant examining various transcripts of the radio broadcast and the ensuing media coverage.

During the small-group work, where students were asked to tackle a set of discussion questions about Bennett's claim, a group of four girls tried to get past their emotional responses. Through the chatter in the classroom, an audible "It was inappropriate!" reverberated from this group, which was situated at the back of the classroom. It was evident that they were attempting to understand Bennett's perspective. One girl, the clear group leader, said, "[Bennett's] sole purpose was to [say that] killing all poverty-stricken babies will reduce crime." The other students in the group responded with "no," offering their own feelings for saying "no" to Bennett and his position, rather than responding to the point made by their classmate. The same group leader attempted to move the group toward an understanding of Bennett's perspective by highlighting the assumption made about eradication of an entire race as a solution to crime, stating, "Bennett could have said it's morally wrong. End of sentence. But he didn't."

During this point in the discussion, the group's feelings about the claim were validated, in that the group leader clarified that Bennett had made it clear, in responses to this claim, that aborting every Black baby would be morally wrong, but he did not explicitly state that in the initial claim he presented during the radio broadcast. Clearly this student felt that calling the action reprehensible did not relieve him from responsibility for putting the solution out there and for not stating strongly enough its moral wrongness. Thus, in an attempt to move the group toward taking up an alternative perspective, this group leader expressed emotional and visceral responses yet developed an understanding of the taken-for-granted assumption of abortion of the Black race as a solution to the problem of crime through a rephrasing of the argument.

This benefits of this exercise are that (1) it enabled students to identify points of view and how those points of view are embedded in a belief system; (2) it forced students to go beyond the literal meanings of the text; and (3) it pushed their thinking forward beyond their initial visceral response, toward a process of interpreting and unpacking the issues implicit within the text.

To propel this interrogation, students grappled for the duration of the unit with the dilemma of facing the claim as an instance of narrative retelling of the official text, which here is Bennett's claim put forth by the instructor—who has set up the claim in a way that anticipates a certain response from the students. The main instructional goal was to propel students into (1) laying claim to and telling their own counterargument narrative responses, and (2) recognizing how points of view can be framed and they themselves can frame others.

Students interrogated the arguments, Bennett's and those created by the students themselves in response, as oral texts, enabling the students to begin to draw from their own cultural understandings of language, participation, and power in order to lay the foundations for responding beyond the affective. Let's consider the small group of girls mentioned above. In an extension of the oral text they created as a response to Bennett (i.e., highlighting the taken-for-granted assumption about aborting the Black race and crime as an alternative to the claim presented by Bennett), these students employed a tool frequently used by their teacher and others in their community, the use of simile and metaphor, to make meaning of an idea or concept. The group leader brought up the notion of cheating, a common and easily understood phenomenon among students their age, by stating that Bennett's argument was "like cheating [because] it's like saying you shouldn't cheat, but not explicitly saying it's wrong, it's immoral, [and] it should not happen." In presenting this metaphor to the group, this student was attempting to elucidate the reasoning Bennett used to lead listeners of his radio broadcast to similar conclusions. In processing this metaphor, this group was attempting to understand Bennett's motives embedded in the argument, his "train of reasoning."

As teacher, I attempted to allow the students to develop their narrative of Bennett's argument, as this literary device presented a clear connection between Bennett's claim and how it spoke to them as students in general, and African American students in particular. I intervened in this discussion and asked whether Bennett backed up his argument sufficiently, to which the group responded with a resounding "no." One of the group members stated, "A lot of people actually believe that Black people cause a lot of crime," to which I reiterated to the group the conclusion they had already reached, "That is why Bennett said that." This use of narrative as a way to work out understandings of complex claims would occur throughout the unit.

Through shared understandings students were able to see how statements or text, by default, position them as readers and, as in this case, subjects of this text. They are able to see how power operates through language, specifically how they are labeled and represented to a larger audience. However, through the process of socially working through the text, enacting it and their readings of it, students were able to reposition themselves in relation to that text and to reposition how they responded to it in socially and academically productive ways. This structure allowed students to enact roles as opposed to being positioned within them, with narrative telling acting as a literacy tool that in turn helped them cope with this act of being forcefully and succinctly positioned by one glib statement.

In the context of taking up complex literary and life texts, both the structure and content of talk play a significant role in framing and creating context and unveiling positionings and thinking of speakers, as social actors, while simultaneously unveiling the ideologies and institutional assumptions inherent in those positionings. Students bring familiarity and various levels of expertise and understanding of this "talk" to generate and unpack complicated readings of texts. As stated in both Chapters 2 and 4, it is within a process orientation that we can view a dualism with regard to norms for talk.

In the classroom, this dualism involved norms for talk that were similar to those found within the discourse in the hair salon and those found within the discipline of responses to literature. For example, in the following inquiry writing assignment, in which students were asked to identify resources of data that would either support or refute Bennett's claim, the student has appropriated the academic language of argument to address particular points. However, she does not directly respond to Bennett. Rather, she problematizes Bennett's claim by addressing larger issues of media sources, power, and representation.

> Bennett's argument is based upon factual evidence from the media
> when he stated that the crime rate in America will go down if more
> Black babies will be (should be) aborted. Bennett is influenced by
> the facts that the media sends out. For example, the media, such as
> the news, depict images that only make light of the poverty level and
> crime in America and how African Americans are the major contribu-
> tions. He thinks that if more Black babies are aborted the crime rate
> would go down.

In her attempts to take up Bennett's argument, the student appropriates the domain-specific language, the language of the discourse. This allows the student to engage not only with her classmates but with Bennett, as she enters into the language of his discourse. Furthermore, this treatment of the claim through language shifting is the result of an analysis being made by the student, as a kind of expert and participant with Bennett as he embodies the full argument. From a procedural orientation view, the primary task is the dualism of attending to multiple discourses, not just one, with norms for talk as the primary instrument.

For this student, this complex construction of self, with the interrelated identities of capable student, member of society, and engager of Bennett, is to the student's benefit as she moves across similar texts. The tools she draws upon include ways of speaking, performing, and reasoning, and constitute transformations within the classroom—not just of talk, but also of self. In other words, as she participates in the activity within the classroom through the use of such tools and resources, she transforms, taking on roles, identities, and participant statuses within the participation framework of the classroom and Bennett's argument. Accordingly, talk moves beyond constituting the problem task to constituting the "guidance" referred to in Rogoff's (1995) concept of guided participation: the cultural and social device that directs the activities of the participants and their subsequent roles within the broader culture of the African American community.

As an additional exercise in taking up alternative perspectives, students were told to take the positioning of Bennett and locate potential justifications for his claim, if indeed they could. To foster this position taking, students were grouped into pairs and given the task of gathering data to support the hypothesis presented by Bennett. The most fundamental is the recognition that there is something to find out, in other words, the understanding that the data being examined can be analyzed and interpreted in a manner that will bear on the claims under consideration. The differing epistemological status of the two claims and evidence must be recognized. This distinction between theory (what makes sense to me) and evidence, as sources of knowing, is essential to maintain or it becomes impossible to construct relations between them (Kuhn, 2005).

This exercise encouraged students to take on an alternative position. I believe that this allows for: (1) an engagement in culturally familiar, problem-solving strategies; (2) the sharing of multiple points of view; (2) the exploration of epistemological roles within the discourse; (3) generation of readings of texts (both socially constructed oral texts and written texts) that account for alternative perspectives; (4) generation of proactive "coping" responses—as opposed, but sometimes in addition, to reactive—to socially and academically threatening mechanisms; and (5) extension beyond the intended participation structure within the classroom.

Additionally, these participation structures are enacted through the discourse of Shoptalk, which accounts for students' readings of events *and* modes of learning through pedagogical practices that attempt to be culturally responsive, not assumptive. This means that what is encouraged through Shoptalk is the availability of a problem-solving process that anticipates students' contributions of their worldviews, in relation to what they experience and what they understand, as a part of that problem-solving equation.

One aspect of this equation is the overlap that exists between culturally situated strategies and those that are specific to domain-based problem solving. In the excerpt from one student's final writing exercise below (a personal letter to Bennett), he points out attitudes that are reflected in the statement Bennett made. He reads the statement not just for what Bennett is literally saying, but the attitudes, values, and ideas instantiated by that claim. Thus, he is attempting to access the nonliteral meanings of the text:

> Dear Bennett,
>   . . . To me your statement was a philosophically insensitive remark made with ignorance of the sensitivity towards a minority ethnic group. What leaves me still skeptical about your statement is your emphasis on the fact that such an inhuman action such as this would work. If you already mentioned that this act would be morally reprehensible why reiterate that it would work? Were you trying to make a quiet stab at African Americans and enlighten racist individuals (not you of course) with your notion? What also infuriated me was your direct correlation between African Americans and crime. Though you meant no harm in your comment your hypothesis does not directly reflect your opinion towards minorities. The timing in which to make this remark was off as well as your decision in expressing this barbaric, thoughtless act.

One could easily begin "assessing" this letter (presented here in part) with a traditional rubric based on abstract conceptions of good letter writing and language–arts–esque forms of argumentation. To do so, however, would miss the point entirely. It is considerably less important to note the "incorrect" salutation, than to consider the ways this student argues for what he believes in ways that the chosen audience—with whom he vehemently disagrees—can hear him.

The author of the letter begins, not with an argument for or against the claim made by Bennett, but rather with an assertion of an ethical position. This rhetorical strategy is not generally developed in traditional language arts conceptions of "argument" because it cannot be "supported" with evidence or data. The student, however, rightly begins with the meat of the problem, which is that the comment was made without "sensitivity towards a minority ethnic group." Furthermore, the student insists, before addressing the warrants of Bennett's claim, that attention be paid to the "inhuman action" that Bennett suggests. Indeed, the student points out that even if the warrants to Bennett's claim were to, somehow, hold up under scrutiny—even if it "would work"—it would still be "morally reprehensible" and "barbaric" beyond mention.

Given the utter vileness of the suggestion, warrants notwithstanding, the statement could be made only for rhetorical purposes, specifically establishing a "direct correlation between African Americans and crime." This kind of statement would have the effect of "enlightening," which could be understood as teaching, racist individuals. The student also takes up the complicated rhetorical strategy of, ironically, setting Bennett up as a benevolent idiot, rather than an amoral monster. The author pretends to understand that Bennett is merely "insensitive," and uses irony with his assertion that Bennett "meant no harm," and is not racist ("not you of course"), and that the comment about aborting all the Black babies "does not directly reflect your opinion towards minorities." Simultaneously, the author paints himself as a neutral, dispassionate critic, using subdued words like *insensitive, skeptical,* and *quiet* to mask his degree of anger, which is revealed with the single word *infuriated*. This strategy reflects the appropriation of the pseudo-rational, media-savvy discourse community into which he is entering with this letter, but it also draws upon AAE strategies of signifying. Together, the message he crafts is both subtle and searing.

In the end, the student produced a text that subverts and escapes the frame of claims and warrants, and keeps the argument where it belongs— making plain the reprehensible nature of the remark and shaming Bennett for uttering it. This is in many ways more sophisticated, and more effective, than prescribed templates for argumentation—and while it is not a model of form and mechanics, it successfully appropriates enough "formal" English to be "credible" to his audience.

CHAPTER 9

Conclusion

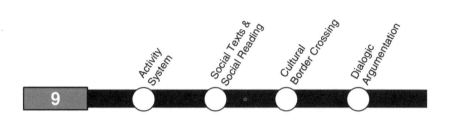

Knowing Where You've Been to Know Where you are Going

While others have argued for the importance of community-based discourse patterns to classroom instruction (Au, 1980; Foster, 1989; Philips, 1972; Tharp & Gallimore, 1988), this study is unique in bringing together insights from two distinct discourse communities to address an overarching issue that should be relevant to all who are concerned with leveraging non-"mainstream" skills for academic development. Such tools move across space and time and can be leveraged for academic development, as "we can show students how to use literacy [which includes reading and composing of social texts], to engage in comparisons and understandings of other possible worlds, other discourses and ideologies" (Luke, 2003, p. 21).

The skill of reading social relations within texts is one that can be harnessed and should be acknowledged and cultivated by teachers of linguistic and cultural minority students. Why? Although members of historically oppressed and marginalized groups may be skillful readers of social relations and sophisticated problem-solvers in community-based contexts, too often they do not experience success at navigating the processes of reconstructing texts in school. When their linguistic, social, and cultural toolkits are recognized, they too often are superficially valorized and viewed as localized, impermeable, and able to be harnessed only within contexts rather than across them. The process of alignment creates opportunities for students to make connections between what they know and what schools want them to learn. This alignment widens the door for demonstrations of academic identities. Students can be members of a school-based disciplinary community while still drawing on points of view, analogies, metaphors, belief systems, and ways of reading that are part of their everyday lives. By investigating the social and arguably academic work participants do in their everyday lives, my hope is to facilitate more conversations between researchers from the disciplines of anthropology, linguistics, and education, as well as between those who work within universities, classrooms, and everyday settings.

Looking across both the hair salon and the language arts classroom, several features stand out. First, through an analysis of both the participation structure in the classroom and the participation framework of the salon, participants organized talk around similar patterns and structural arrangements of interaction. In both the classroom and salon, participants incorporated discursive rules of participation in both turn taking and narrative performance, which bear a crucial relationship to the history of African American Vernacular English discourse and norms for participation that are a part of the African American storytelling tradition and are recognizable across both time and space by members of that community.

Second, in both the classroom and the hair salon, meaning-making occurred within a framework that consisted of the use of AAE as a tool. An analysis of argumentation structures reveals how language contributed to the telling of action as well as how individuals co-constructed meaning and understood those actions as having some meaning. Furthermore, in the classroom, the implementation of a culturally relevant method of interaction not only allowed the students to work through a shared cultural past, but also situated their understanding and interpretations of texts, oral and written, within a cultural paradigm that makes use of the rules, values, and beliefs that are an extension of a shared primary discourse (Gee, 1997).

As members of the African American cultural community, many urban high school students develop with and through the kinds of routine, problem-solving strategies that both occur in the salon and characterize their social space as a community of practice. Such practices, like ways of participating, speaking, valuing, believing, and arguing, have affordances for the kinds of things that many English teachers want all students to do—to understand what texts mean and how texts mean.

Those concerned with leveraging the out-of-school practices of students of color for in-school literacy learning have argued frequently that "students should be empowered" to bring their personal (cultural) ways of knowing to the fore of classroom learning (Lee, in King, 2005; Rosenblatt, 1978). This view attempts to underscore and challenge the dominant theme in education, which views students' cultural practices as deficits rather than as resources. Most recent reform efforts, particularly at the secondary literacy level, have focused a great deal on making use of the cognitive research on reading to enhance curriculum on teaching those reading comprehension strategies that characterize "good readers" (Lee, 2005).

In literacy education, for example, struggling readers often do not understand what good readers do. Rather, they understand whether they are good readers or bad readers, and that the ultimate goal of "good reading" is one to be desired. Such reforms have generated and maintained (1) ethnocentric and often assumptive representations of multiculturalism; (2) only superficial consideration of students' responses to themes in a work; and (3) little empirical representation of how those responses are situated in the beliefs, value systems, and practices of the cultures to which the students belong.

The gifting of empowerment, instantiated in the belief that students come to the classroom powerless, too often tends to be the goal of many classrooms when it comes to educating students of color. Furthermore, such a view maintains the privilege of the teacher as the authority figure, dictating what means are appropriate and necessary to learning. Thus, Martin Luther King, Jr., as a revered text figure, is celebrated in school as a folk hero who fought for something that perhaps has been overcome. While on the other hand, Malcolm X, as a demonized text figure, rarely is mentioned within the canon of multicultural literature—or, if there is mention, it is only in stark contrast to MLK, as a menacing race-badgering militant (Majors & Ansari, 2009).

This orientation does several things. First, it creates a "food," "folks," and "festivals" mentality—that culture can be diluted down to its ethnic food, its folk heroes from history, and select safe, nonthreatening festivals celebrating culture. Second, it upholds the teacher as the depositor and gatekeeper of knowledge, where the students are empty vessels, or worse, misinformed about cultural themes. Third, it does not take into account the organic nature of culture as an aspect of activity systems that students participate in and create every day; rather, culture is presented to students as occurring within a vacuum, packaged to be handed over. Fourth, empowerment is akin to "feeling good" in teacher-derived space. The fact that the teacher finds the space safe and comfortable does not justify an assumption that it thus creates comfort and self-actualization for the students. Such a space is rarely one that is meant to be engaged in or critical of new meanings and how these are taken up in students' lived lives as they read the world and the word.

Culture thus is something to be consumed, and empowerment is the by-product of consumption. Such an orientation omits the fact that learning how to figure out the themes in a work, even one that is intentionally "multicultural," is more empowering than seeing oneself in a work. This approach reinforces the status quo, still drawing attention to difference as deficit; what is supposed to be a transformative curriculum merely is the same old, same old.

For example, recent arguments regarding the problem-solving resources of children from diverse backgrounds as being "useful but different" from those central to domain-based, problem-solving inquiry lead to the conclusion that this difference is a barrier to learning that must be overcome. While some have made the argument that seeing oneself within text can empower a reader, others have countered that "if readers cannot make sense of the work, they are likely to have either a negative personal response to the work or at best a very unembellished one" (Lee, 2007, p. 64).

In framing the actions of African American participants of discourse in this way, I am accounting for the *mediational role of literacy practices in community contexts*. I also am accounting for the role of participating members of these communities not just as active participants who are viewed as being in resistance to literate practices, but as active teachers and learners who use such practices in culturally responsive, authentic ways. Such an account disrupts deficit models and provides insight into alternative spaces for harnessing valuable skills for teaching and learning. As such, there are various conceptualizations of literacy that are taken up through our work in the language arts classroom, particularly in urban communities.

Progressive educators concerned with leveraging the out-of-school practices of students of color for in-school literacy learning have argued frequently that students should be empowered to bring their personal (cultural) ways of knowing to the fore of classroom learning (Lee in King, 2005; Rosenblatt, 1978). This argument attempts to underscore and challenge the dominant theme in education, which either (1) views students' cultural practices (e.g., ways of speaking, communicating, listening, responding) as deficits rather than as resources, or (2) tends to link popular cultural practices, such as rap and hip-hop music, to classroom practices without making explicit how and where such links occur. From either of these views, cultural practices are akin to music and entertainment and not problem-solving processes.

As previously stated, recent literacy reform efforts, particularly at the secondary school level where literacy typically is dealt with within the domain of responses to literature, have focused on making use of cognitive research on reading to enhance curriculum for teaching those reading comprehension strategies that characterize good readers of literary texts (Lee, 2007). One problem that I see with this approach, however, is that struggling adolescent readers, Black and White, often do not understand what good, expert readers of literature do (Rabinowitz, 1987).

Shoptalk in the classroom moves beyond an explication of discourse analysis and recognizes the importance of making use of that which is produced within cultures and to which students have access and bring into the classroom. However, it also recognizes and argues for the understanding of the knowledge produced within that culture and knowing how to produce and therefore critique that knowledge (Moje, 2007). This knowledge is part of a dual consciousness generated within students as members of their community, one in which they are socialized into familiarity with the language and manners of a larger dominant society, while developing a self-defined standpoint from which to respond.

Notes

Introduction

1. Pseudonyms are used throughout to protect the identities of the participants.

Chapter 2

1. Building on the sociocultural argument of human development (that the activity setting and the interactions with others and with artifacts available as part of the practices of that setting mediate mental functioning), Rogoff adds a more detailed dimension to this argument by proposing three interrelated planes on which to view, understand, and analyze human mental functioning: (1) apprenticeship, (2) guided participation, and (3) participatory appropriation. Apprenticeship is defined as a set of social practices that are inherited over time. These social practices are intended both to induct novices into an established community of practice and to define the ways of reasoning that characterize participation in the practice, as well as the artifacts and tools that are used in the practice (Lee & Majors, 2003).

Chapter 3

1. In identifying skills in the performance of work tasks, we also account for manual skills, such as dexterity or coordination, especially in the execution of learned physical tasks.

Chapter 7

1. This section is drawn from Lee and Majors (2000) *Cultural Modeling's Response to Rogoff's Challenge: Understanding Apprenticeship, Guided Participation and Participatory Appropriation in a Culturally Responsive, Subject Matter Specific Context*. Paper presented at the Annual Meeting of the American Educational Research Association, April, 2000.

2. I do not mean to suggest that literary critics and serious readers of canonical literature approach texts in exactly the same manner. This is not the case. However, there is an intellectual terrain that they share around what constitutes serious versus purely popular literature. They share a common interest in aesthetic qualities of the work in addition to what the work implies about the human condition. I put these two communities of readers together to suggest that what they share as approaches to reading is what schools attempt to teach.

References

Abrahams, R. D. (1976). The complex relations of simple forms. In D. Bon-Amos (Ed.), *Folklore genres* (pp. 193–214). Austin, TX: University of Texas Press.

Agre, P. (1997). How to train novice computer users. *Training, 34*(3), 7.

Anyon, J. (1980). Social class and the hidden curriculum of work. *Journal of Education, 162,* 67–92.

Anzaldua, G. (1987). *Borderlands/La frontera: The new mestiza.* San Francisco, CA: Aunt Lute Books.

Arnett, J. J. (1995). Broad and narrow socialization: The family in the context of a cultural theory. *Journal of Marriage and the Family, 57,* 617–628.

Au, K. (1980). Participation structures in a reading lesson with Hawaiian children: Analysis of a culturally appropriate instructional event. *Anthropology and Education Quarterly, 11,* 91–115.

Bakhtin, M. (1981). *The dialogic imagination: Four essays* (M. Holquist, Ed., C. Emerson & M. Holquist, Trans.). Austin, TX: University of Texas Press.

Bakhtin, M. (1986). *Speech genres and other late essays.* Austin, TX: University of Texas Press.

Banks, J. A. (1998). Curriculum transformation. In J. A. Banks (Ed.), *An introduction to multicultural education* (2nd ed., pp. 21–34). Boston, MA: Allyn & Bacon.

Banks, J. A. (2001). Citizenship education and diversity: Implications for teacher education. *Journal of Teacher Education, 52,* 5–16.

Banks, J. A. (2003). Teaching literacy for social justice and global citizenship. *Language Arts, 81,* 18–19.

Barley, S. R., & Orr, J. E. (Eds.) (1997). *Between craft and science: Technical work in U.S. settings.* Ithaca, NY: Cornell University Press.

Barton, D., & Hamilton, M. (1998). *Local literacies: Reading and writing in one classroom.* London, UK: Routledge.

Barton, D., Hamilton, M., & Ivanic, R. (2003) *Situated literacies: Reading and writing in context.* London, UK: Routledge.

Bell, D. (1995). Who's afraid of critical race theory. *U. Ill. L. Rev.,* 893.

Bell, D. (2004). *Silent covenants.* Oxford, UK: Oxford University Press.

Bennett, W. (2005, September 28). *Morning in America* [Radio broadcast]. Washington, DC: SRN.

Berliner, P. (1994). *Thinking in jazz: The infinite art of improvisation.* Chicago, IL: The University of Chicago Press.

Bomer, R. et al. (2008). Miseducating teachers about the poor: A critical analysis of Ruby Payne's claims about poverty. *Teachers College Record 110*(12), 2497–2531.

Booth, W. C. (1974). *A rhetoric of irony* (Vol. 641). Chicago, IL: University of Chicago Press.

Bourdieu, P. (1977). *Outline of a theory of practice* (Vol. 16). New York, NY: Cambridge university press.

Bourdieu, P., & Thompson, J. B. (1991). *Language and symbolic power.* Cambridge, MA: Harvard University Press.

Bowman, P. J., & Howard, C. (1985). Race related socialization, motivation, and academic achievement: A study of Black youths in three generation families. *Journal of the American Academy of Child Psychiatry, 24*, 134–141.

Boykin, A. W., & Ellison, C. M. (1995). The multiple ecologies of Black youth socialization: An Afrographic analysis. In R. L. Taylor (Ed.), *African American youth: Their social and economic status in the United States* (pp. 93–112). Westport, CT: Praeger.

Bransford, J., Brown, A., & Cocking, R. (Eds.) (2000). *How people learn.* Washington DC: National Academy Press.

Breier, M. (2005). A disciplinary-specific approach to the recognition of prior informal experience in adult pedagogy. *Studies in Continuing Education, 27*(1), 51–65.

Brown v. Board of Education of Topeka, 347 U.S. 483 (1954).

Brown, J. S., & Duguid, P. (1991). Organizational learning and communities-of-practice: Toward a unified view of working, learning, and innovation. *Organization Science, 2*(1), 40–57.

Bruner, J. (1990). *Acts of meaning.* Cambridge, MA: Harvard University Press.

Coard, S. I., Wallace, S. A., Stevenson, H. C., & Brotman, L. M. (2004). Towards culturally relevant interventions: The consideration of racial socialization in parent training with African American families. *Journal of Child and Family Studies, 13*(3), 277–293.

Cole, M. (1996). *Cultural psychology: A once and future discipline.* Cambridge, MA: Belknap Press of Harvard University Press.

Crenshaw, K., Gotanda, N., Peller, G., & Thomas, K. (Eds.). (1995). *Critical race theory: The key writings that formed the movement.* New York, NY: New Press.

Cresswell, J. W. (2003). *Research design: Qualitative, quantitative, and mixed methods approaches.* Thousand Oaks, CA: Sage Publications.

Darling-Hammond, L. (2010). *The flat world and education: How America's commitment to equity will determine our future.* New York, NY: Teachers College Press.

Delgado, R., & Stefancic, J. (Eds.). (2000). *Critical race theory: The cutting edge.* (2nd ed.). Philadelphia, PA: Temple University Press.

Delpit, L. (1995). *Other people's children: Cultural conflict in the classroom.* New York, NY: New Press.

Dirkx, J. (1996). Human resource development as adult education: Fostering the educative workplace. In R. W. Rowden (Ed.), *Workplace learning: Debating five critical questions of theory and practice: Vol. 72. New directions for adult and continuing education* (pp. 41–47). San Francisco, CA: Jossey-Bass.

Duranti, A. (1997). *Linguistic anthropology.* Cambridge, UK: Cambridge University Press.

Ellison, R. (1999). Richard Wright's blues. *The Antioch Review, 57*(3), 263–276.

Erickson, F., & Mohatt, G. (1982). The cultural organization of participation structures in two classrooms of Indian students. In G. Spindler (Ed.), *Doing the ethnography of schooling: Educational anthropology in action* (pp. 132–174) . New York, NY: Holt, Rinehart and Winston.

Fairclough, N. (1995). *Critical discourse analysis: The critical study of language.* New York, NY: Longman.

Fanon, F. (1967). *Black skin, white masks.* (C. Markmann, trans.). New York, NY: Grove Press.

Fanon, F. (2004). *The wretched of the earth* (R. Philcox, Trans.). New York: Grove Press.

Fillmore, L. W. (1991). When learning a second language means losing the first. *Early Childhood Research Quarterly, 6,* 323–346.

Fine, M. (1994). Working the hyphens: Reinventing self and other in qualitative research. In N. K. Denizen & Y. S. Lincoln (Eds.), *Handbook of qualitative research* (pp. 70–82). Thousand Oaks, CA: Sage.

Foster, M. (1989). "It's cookin' now": A performance analysis of the speech events of a Black teacher in an urban community college. *Language in Society, 18*(01), 1–29.

Foucault, M. (1980). *Power/knowledge: Selected interviews and other writings.* Brighton, UK: Harvester Press.

Kazembe, L. (2012). *Beyond Nommo: Contextualizing the literary geneology of the black arts movement.* Doctoral dissertation, The University of Illinois, Chicago.

Frabutt, J., Walker, A. M., & MacKinnon-Lewis, C. (2002). Racial socialization messages and the quality of mother/child interactions in African American families. *Journal of Early Adolescence, 22*(2), 200–217.

Fraser, N. (1989). Rethinking the public sphere: A contribution to the critique of actually existing democracy. In C. Calhoun (Ed.), *Habermas and the public sphere.* Cambridge, MA: MIT Press.

Freire, P. (1993). *Pedagogy of the oppressed* (M. Ramos, trans.). New York, NY: Continuum.

Gates Jr., H. L. (1994). In the kitchen. *New Yorker, 82–86.*

Gay, G. (2000). *Culturally responsive teaching: Theory, research, and practice.* New York, NY: Teachers College Press.

Gee, J. P. (1992). *Sociolinguistics and literacies.* New York, NY: Falmer Press.

Gee, J. P. (1993). Postmodernism and literacies. In C. Lankshear & P. L. McLaren (Eds.), *Critical literacy: Politics, praxis and the postmodern* (pp. 271–295). New York, NY: State University of New York.

Gee, J. P. (1997). *The social mind: Language, ideology, and social practice.* New York, NY: Bergin and Garvey.

Gee, J.P (2000). Identity as an analytic lens for research in education. *Review of Educational Research, 25,* 99–125. Washington, DC: American Educational Research Association.

Gee, J. P., Hull, G., & Lankshear, C. (1996). *The new work order: Behind the language of the new capitalism.* Boulder, CO: Westview Press.

Gilbert, P. (1992). Narrative as gendered social practice: In search of different story lines for language research. *Linguistics and Education, 5,* 211–218.

Goffman, E. (1969). *Strategic interaction.* Philadelphia, PA: University of Pennsylvania Press.

Goffman, E. (1974). *Frame analysis.* New York, NY: HarperCollins.

Goffman, E. (1981). *Forms of talk.* Philadelphia, PA: University of Pennsylvania Press.

Gomez, K., & Pinkard, N. (2014). *The digital youth network: Cultivating digital media citizenship in urban communities.* Cambridge, MA: MIT Press.

Gramski, A. (1971). *Selections from the prison notebooks* (Q. Hoare, Ed. & G. Nowell-Smith, Trans.). London, UK: Lawrence & Wishart.

Graves, B., & Frederiksen, C. H. (1996) A cognitive study of literary expertise. In R. J. Kruez & M. S. Macnealy (Eds.), *Empirical approaches to literature and aesthetics* (pp. 397–418). Norwood, NJ: Ablex.

Grimes, J. E. (1975). *The thread of discourse.* Ann Arbor, MI: University of Michigan Press.

Guinier, L., & Torres, G. (2002). *The miner's canary: Enlisting race, resisting power, transforming democracy.* Cambridge, MA: Harvard University Press.

Gumperz, J. (1982). *Discourse strategies.* Cambridge, UK: Cambridge University Press.

Gumperz, J. (1996). Conversational inference. *Rethinking linguistic relativity,* (17), 374.

Gutierrez, K. D., Baquedano-Lopez, P., Tejeda, C., & Rivera, A. (1999, April). *Hybridity as a tool for understanding literacy learning: Building on a syncretic approach.* Paper presented at the annual meeting of the American Association of Educational Research, Montreal, Canada.

Gutierrez, K. D., & Rogoff, B. (2003). Cultural ways of learning: Individual traits or repertoires of practice. *Educational Researcher, 32*(5), 19–25.

Gutierrez, K. D., Rymes, B., & Larson, J. (1995). Script, counterscript, and underlife in the classroom: James Brown versus Brown v. Board of Education. *Harvard Educational Review, 65,* 445–471.

Hale, Thomas, A. (2007). *Griots and griottes: Masters of words and music (African expressive cultures).* Bloomington, IN: Indiana University Press.

Hamilton, M. (2006). Just do it: Literacies, everyday learning and the irrelevance of pedagogy. *Studies in the Education of Adults, 38*(2), 125–140.

Harding, S. (1987). Introduction: Is there a feminist method? In S. Harding (Ed.), *Feminism and methodology* (pp. 1–14). Bloomington, IN: Indiana University Press.

Harris-Lacewell, M. V. (2004). *Barbershops, bibles, and BET: Everyday talk and Black political thought.* Princeton, NJ: Princeton University Press.

Hill-Collins, P. (2000). *Black feminist thought: Knowledge, consciousness, and the politics of empowerment.* New York, NY: Routledge.

Hilliard, A. G. (1995). *The maroon within us: Selected essays on African American community socialization*. Baltimore, MD: Black Classic Press.

Hillocks, G. (1982). Inquiry and the composing process: Theory and research. *College English, 659–673*.

Hillocks, G. (2011). *Teaching argument writing: Grades 6–12*. Portsmouth, NH: Heinemann.

Hollins, E. R. (1996). *Culture in school learning: Revealing the deep meaning*. Mahwah, NJ: Erlbaum.

hooks, b. (2010). *Teaching critical thinking: Practical wisdom*. New York, NY: Routledge.

hooks, b. (2014). *Teaching to transgress*. Routledge.

Hughes, D., & Chen, L. (1999). The nature of parents' race-related communications to children: A developmental perspective. In L. Balter & C. S. Tamis-LeMonda (Eds.), *Child psychology: A handbook of contemporary issues* (pp. 467–490). Philadelphia, PA: Taylor & Francis.

Hughes, S. A., & North, C. E. (2012). Beyond popular cultural and structural arguments imagining a compass to guide burgeoning urban achievement gap scholars. *Education and Urban Society 44*(3), 274–293.

Hull, G., & Schultz, K. (Eds.). (2002). *School's out! Bridging out-of-school literacies with classroom practice*. New York, NY: Teachers College Press.

Hutchins, E. (1996). Learning to navigate. In S. Chaiklin & J. Lave (Eds.), *Understanding practice: Perspectives on activity and context* (pp. 35–63). Cambridge, MA: Cambridge University Press.

Jacobs-Huey, L. (1996). Negotiating price in an African American beauty salon. *Issues in Applied Linguistics, 7*(1), 45–59.

Jacobs-Huey, L. (1997a). Is there an authentic African American speech community: Carla revisited. *U. Penn Working Papers in Linguistics, 4*(1), 331–370.

Jacobs-Huey, L. (1997b). "We are just like doctors, . . . we heal sick hair": Professional and cultural discourses of hair and identity in a Black hair care seminar. *Salsa V, 39*, 213–233.

Jacobs-Huey, L. (2006). *From the kitchen to the parlor: language and becoming in African American women's hair care*. New York, NY: Oxford University Press.

Kazembe, L. (2012). *Beyond Nommo: Contextualizing the literary genealogy of the Black arts movement* (Unpublished doctoral dissertation). University of Illinois, Chicago.

Keating, D., & Sasse, D. (1996). Cognitive socialization in adolescence: Critical period for a critical habit of mind. In G. R. Adams, R. Montemayor, & T. Gullota (Eds.), *Psychosocial development during adolescence: Progress in developmental contextualism* (pp. 232–259). NewYork, NY: Sage.

King, J. E. (2005). A transformative vision of Black education for human freedom. In J. E. King (Ed.), *Black education: A transformative research and action agenda for the new century* (pp. 3–18). Mahwah, NJ: Erlbaum.

Kochman, T. (1981). *Black and White styles in conflict*. Chicago, IL: University of Chicago Press.

Kozol, J. (2012). *Savage inequalities: Children in America's schools.* New York: Broadway Books.

Kuhn, D. (1991). *The skills of argument.* New York, NY: Cambridge University Press.

Kuhn, D. (2000). Metacognitive development. *Current Directions in Psychological Science, 9*(5), 178–181.

Kuhn, D. (2005). *Education for thinking.* Cambridge, MA: Harvard University Press.

Kuhn, D. (2015). Thinking together and alone. *Educational Researcher, 44*(1), 46–53.

Kuhn, D., & Crowell, A. (2011). Dialogic argumentation as a vehicle for developing young adolescents' thinking. *Psychological Science, 22*(4), 545–552.

Ladson-Billings, G. J., & Donnor, J. K. (2005). Waiting for the call: The moral activist role of critical race theory scholarship. In N. K. Denzin & Y. S. Lincoln (Eds.), *Handbook of qualitative research* (3rd, ed., pp. 279–301). Thousand Oaks, CA: Sage.

Labov, W. (1972). *Language in the inner city: Studies in the Black English vernacular.* Philadelphia, PA: University of Pennsylvania Press.

Lampert, M. (1990). When the problem is not the question and the solution is not the answer: Mathematical knowing and teaching. *American Educational Research Journal, 27*(1), 29–64.

Langer, J. A. (1987). *A sociocognitive perspective on literacy learning.* Norwood, NJ: Ablex.

Lankshear, C. (1997). *Changing literacies.* Buckingham, UK: Open University Press.

Lave, J. (1996). The practice of learning. In S. Chaiklin & J. Lave (Eds.), *Understanding practice: Perspectives on activity and context* (pp. 3–32). Cambridge, MA: Cambridge University Press.

Lave, J., & Wenger, E. (1991). *Situated learning: Legitimate peripheral participation.* Cambridge, UK: Cambridge University Press.

Lee, C. D. (1992). Literacy, cultural diversity, and instruction. *Education & Urban Society, 24,* 279–291.

Lee, C. D. (1993). *Signifying as a scaffold for literary interpretation: The pedagogical implications of an African American discourse genre.* Urbana, IL: National Council of Teachers of English.

Lee, C. D. (1995). A culturally based cognitive apprenticeship: Teaching African-American high school students' skills in literary interpretation. *Reading Research Quarterly, 30*(4), 608–631.

Lee, C. D. (2005). Intervention research based on current views of cognition and learning. In J. King (Ed.), *Black education: A transformative research and action agenda for the new century* (pp. 73–114). Mahwah, NJ: Erlbaum.

Lee, C. D. (2007). *Culture, literacy, and learning: Taking bloom in the midst of the whirlwind.* New York, NY: Teachers College Press.

Lee, C. D., & Majors, Y. (2000). *Cultural modeling's response to Rogoff's challenge: Understanding apprenticeship, guided participation and participatory appropriation in a culturally responsive, subject matter specific context.* Paper presented at the Annual Meeting of the American Educational Research Association.

Lee, C. D., & Majors, Y. (2003). Heading up the street: Localized opportunities for shared constructions of knowledge. *Pedagogy, Culture & Society, 11*(1), 49–67.

Lee, C. D., Spencer, M. B., & Harpalani, V. (2003). "Every shut eye ain't sleep": Studying how people live culturally. *Educational Researcher: A Publication of the American Educational Research Association, 32*(5), 6 –13.

Lee, M.Y., & Johnson-Bailey, J. (2004). Challenges to the classroom authority of women of color. *New Directions for Adult and Continuing Education, 106*, 55–64.

Leonardo, Z., & Porter, R. (2010). Pedagogy of fear: Toward a Fanonian theory of "safety" in race dialogue. *Race, Ethnicity and Education, 13*(2), 139–157.

Luff, P., Hindmarsh, J., & Heath, C. (Eds.). (2000). *Workplace studies: Recovering work practice and informing system designs.* Cambridge, UK: Cambridge University Press.

Luke, A. (2003). *Literacy education for a new ethics of global community.* Urbana, IL: National Council of Teachers of English.

Lynn, M. (1999). Toward a critical race pedagogy: A research note. *Urban Education 33,* (5), 606–626.

Majors, Y. (1998). Finding the multi-voiced self: A narrative. *Journal of Adolescent and Adult Literacy, 42*(2), 76–83.

Majors, Y. (2001). Passing mirrors: Subjectivity in a midwestern hair salon. *Anthropology and Education Quarterly, 32*(1), 116–130.

Majors, Y. (2003). Shoptalk: Teaching and learning in an African American hair salon. *Mind, Culture and Activity, 10*(4), 289–310.

Majors, Y. (2004). "'I wasn't scared of them, they were scared of me": Constructions of self/other in a midwestern hair salon. *Anthropology and Education Quarterly, 35*(2), 167–188.

Majors, Y. (2006, November). *Shoptalk in the classroom: The community socialization of African American youth in a language arts class.* Paper presented at the annual convention of the National Council of Teachers of English, Nashville, TN.

Majors, Y. (2007). Narrations of cross-cultural encounters as interpretative frames for reading word and world. *Discourse and Society, 18*(4), 479–505.

Majors, Y. (2014). Joy and the smart kids: Competing ways of being and believing. *Journal of Adolescent and Adult Literacy, 57*(8), 633–641.

Majors, Y., & Ansari, S. (2009). Cultural community practices as urban classroom resources. In L. Tillman (Ed.), *The sage handbook of African American education,* (pp. 107–122). Thousand Oaks, CA: Sage Publications.

Majors, Y., Kim, J., & Ansari, S. (2009). Beyond hip-hop: A cultural context view of literacy. In L. Christenbury, J. Bomer, & P. Smagorinsky (Eds.), *Handbook of adolescent literacy research.* New York, NY: Guilford Publications.

Majors, Y., & Orellana, M. (2003, April). *Envisioning texts or reading the other.* Paper presented at the annual conference of the American Educational Research Association, Chicago, IL.

McAdoo, H. P. (1985). Racial attitude and self-concept of young Black children over time. In H. P. McAdoo & J. L. McAdoo (Eds.), *Black children: Social, educational, and parental environments* (pp. 213–242). Newbury Park, CA: Sage.

McNeil, D. (1999). *Racial versus ethnic socialization: A family ecology approach.* Evanston, IL: Northwestern University Press.

Miller, P. J., Potts, R., Fung, H., Hoogstra, L., & Mintz, J. (1990). Narrative practices and the social construction of self in childhood. *American Ethnologist, 17,* 292–311.

Milner, H. R. (2005). Developing a multicultural curriculum in a predominantly White teaching context: Lessons from an African American teacher in a suburban English classroom. *Curriculum Inquiry, 35*(4), 391–427.

Moje, E. (2007). Developing socially just subject-matter instruction: A review of the literature on disciplinary literacy teaching. *Review of Research in Education, 31,* 1–44.

Moll, L. C. (2000). Inspired by Vygotsky: Ethnographic experiments in education. In C. D. Lee & P. Smagorinsky (Eds.), *Vygotskian perspectives on literacy research: Constructing meaning through collaborative inquiry* (pp. 256–268). New York, NY: Cambridge University Press.

Moll, L., & Greenberg, J. (1990). Creating zones of possibilities: Combining social contexts for instruction. In *Vygotsky and education: Instructional implications and applications of sociohistorical psychology* (pp. 319–348). New York, NY: Cambridge University Press.

Morgan, M. (1998). More than a mood or an attitude: Discourse and verbal genres in African American culture. In S. S. Mufwene, J. R. Rickford, G. Bailey, & Baugh, J. (Eds.), *African-American English: Structure, history, and use* (pp. 251–281). New York, NY: Routledge.

Morrell, E., & Duncan-Andrade, J. (2003). What they do learn in school: Hip-hop as a bridge to canonical poetry. In J. Mahiri (Ed.), *What they don't learn in school: Literacy in the lives of urban youth* (pp. 247–268). New York, NY: Peter Lang.

Murray, C. B., Stokes, J. E., & Peacock, M. J. (1999). Racial socialization of African American children: A review. In R. L. Jones (Ed.), *African American children, youth, and parenting* (pp. 209–229). Hampton, VA: Cobb & Henry.

Muse, J. H. (2010). Flash mobs and the diffusion of audience. *Theater. 40*(3), 9–23.

Nasir, N. (2011). *Racialized identities.* Palo Alto, CA: Stanford University Press.

Ochs, E. (1990). Indexing gender. In A. Duranti & C. Goodwin (Eds.), *Rethinking context: Language as an interactive phenomenon* (pp. 336–358). Cambridge, UK: Cambridge University Press.

Ochs, E., & Capps, L. (2001). *Living narrative: Creating lives in everyday storytelling.* Cambridge, MA: Harvard University Press.

Orr, J. E. (1990). Sharing knowledge, celebrating identity: Community memory in a service culture. In D. S. Middleton & D. Edwards (Eds.), *Collective remembering: Memory in society* (pp. 168–189). Beverly Hills, CA: Sage.

Orr, J. E. (1996). *Talking about machines: An ethnography of a modern job.* Ithaca, NY: Cornell University Press.

Paredes, A. (1984). On ethnographic work among minority groups. In R. Romo & R. Paredes (Eds.), *New directions in Chicano scholarship* (pp. 1–32). Santa Barbara, CA: University of California, Center for Chicano Studies.

Parker, L., & Lynn, M. (2002). What's race got to do with it? Critical race theory's conflicts with and connections to qualitative research methodology and epistemology. *Qualitative Inquiry, 8*(1), 7–22.

Payne, R. K. (2005). *A framework for understanding poverty.* Highlands, TX: aha! Process.

Peters, M. F. (1985). Racial socialization of young Black children. In H. P. McAdoo & J. L. McAdoo (Eds.), *Black children: Social, educational, and parental environments* (pp. 159–173). Newbury Park, CA: Sage.

Phelan, P., Davidson, A., & Cao Yu, H. (1998). *Adolescents' worlds: Negotiating family, peers, and school.* New York, NY: Teachers College Press.

Philips, S. (1972). Participant structures and communicative competence: Warm Springs children in community and classrooms. In C. B. Cazden, V. P. John, & D. Hymes (Eds.), *Functions of language in the classroom* (pp. 320 –394). New York, NY: Teachers College Press.

Piaget, J. (1926). *The language and thought of the child.* London, UK: Kegan Paul.

Rabinowitz, P. (1987). *Before reading: Narrative conventions and the politics of interpretation.* Ithaca, NY: Simon & Schuster.

Republican Platform Committee. (2012). Retrieved from www.gop.com/2012 -republican-platform_home/

Resnick, D., & Resnick, L. (1977). The nature of literacy: An historical exploration. *Harvard Educational Review, 43*, 370–385.

Rogoff, B. (1990). *Apprenticeship in thinking: Cognitive development in social context.* New York, NY: Oxford University Press

Rogoff, B. (1995). Observing sociocultural activity and three planes: Participatory appropriation, guided participation, and apprenticeship. In J. , P. del-Rio, & A. Alvarez (Eds.), *Sociocultural studies of mind* (pp. 139–164). New York, NY: Cambridge University Press.

Rogoff, B. (2003). *The cultural nature of human development.* New York, NY: Oxford University Press.

Rooks, N. (1996) *Hair raising: Beauty, culture, and African American women.* New Brunswick, NJ: Rutgers University Press.

Rose, M. (2001). The working life of a waitress. *Mind, Culture, and Activity, 8,* 3–27.

Rose, M. (2004). *The mind at work.* New York, NY: Viking Books.

Rosenblatt, L. (1978). *The reader, the text, the poem.* Carbondale, IL: Southern Illinois University Press.

Rotherman, M. J., & Phinney, J. S. (1987). Introduction: Definitions and perspectives in the study of children's ethnic socialization. In J. S. Phinney & M. J. Rotherman (Eds.), *Children's ethnic socialization: Pluralism and development* (pp. 10–28). Beverly Hills, CA: Sage.

Schank, R. C., & Abelson, R. (1977). *Scripts, plans, goals, and understanding.* Hillsdale, NJ: Erlbaum.

Scribner, S. (1984). Studying working intelligence. In B. Rogoff & J. Lave (Eds.), *Everyday cognition: Its development in social context* (pp. 9–40). Cambridge, MA: Harvard University Press.

Scribner, S., & Cole, M. (1981). *The psychology of literacy*. Cambridge, MA: Harvard University Press.

Smitherman, G. (1977). *Talkin and testifyin: The language of Black America*. Boston, MA: Houghton Mifflin.

Smitherman, G. (2000). *Talkin that talk: Language, culture and education in African America*. New York, NY: Routledge.

Spencer, M. B. (1983). Children's cultural values and parental child rearing strategies. *Developmental Review, 3*, 351–370.

Spencer, M. B., Swanson, D. P., & Cunningham, M. (1991). Ethnicity, ethnic identity and competence formation: Adolescent transition and cultural transformation. *Journal of Negro Education, 60*, 366–387.

Srivastava, S. (2005). "You're calling me a racist?" The moral and emotional regulation of antiracism and feminism. *Signs: Journal of Women in Culture and Society, 31*(1), 30–62.

Stevenson, H. C., Cameron, R., Herrero-Taylor, T., & Davis, G. Y. (2002). Development of the teenager experience of racial socialization scale: Correlates of race-related socialization frequency from the perspective of Black youth. *Journal of Black Psychology, 28*(2), 84–106.

Stevenson, H. C., & Davis, G. Y. (2004). Racial socialization. In R. Jones (Ed.), *Black psychology* (4th ed., pp. 176–189). Hampton VA: Cobb & Henry.

Stevenson, H. C., Herrero-Taylor, T., Cameron, R., & Davis, G. Y. (2002). "Mitigating instigation": Cultural phenomenological influences of anger and fighting among "big-boned" and "baby-faced" African American youth. *Journal of Youth and Adolescence, 31*(6), 473–485.

Street, B. (2000). New literacies in theory and practice: What are the implications for language in education? *Linguistics in Education, 10*, 1–24.

Swidler, A. (2001). *Talk of love: How culture matters*. Chicago, IL: University of Chicago Press.

Tharp, R., & Gallimore, R. (1988). *Rousing minds to life: Teaching, learning and schooling in social context*. New York, NY: Cambridge University Press.

Thompson, A. (2003). Tiffany, friend of people of color: White investments in antiracism. *International Journal of Qualitative Studies in Education, 16*(1), 7–29.

Van Den Broek, P. W. (1994) Comprehension of narrative texts: Inference processes and the construction of coherence. In M.A. Gersbacher (Ed.), *Handbook of Psycholinguistics* (pp. 539–588). San Diego, CA: Academic Press.

Vygotsky, L. (1978). *Mind in society: The development of higher psychological processes* (M. Cole, V. John-Steiner, S. Scribner, & E. Souberman, Eds.). Cambridge, MA: Harvard University Press.

Wells, G. (2000). Dialogic inquiry in education: Building on the legacy of Vygotsky. In C. D. Lee & P. Smagorinsky (Eds.), *Vygotskian perspectives on literacy research* (pp. 51–84). Cambridge, UK: Cambridge University Press.

Wertsch, J. (1985). *Vygotsky and the social formation of mind*. Cambridge, MA: Harvard University Press.

Wertsch, J. (1993). *Voices of the mind*. Cambridge, MA: Harvard University Press.

Wertsch, J., del Rio, P., & Alvarez, A. (Eds.). (1995). *Sociocultural studies of mind*. New York, NY: Cambridge University Press.

Wodak, R. (1996). *Disorders of discourse*. London, UK: Longman.

Wodak, R., & Meyer, M. (Eds.). (2001). *Methods of critical discourse analysis*. London, UK: Sage.

Index

Abelson, R., 28, 48
Abrahams, R. D., 4
Activity systems, 24–27
Addie, Ms. (hair salon client), 1–2, 4, 6–7, 9, 19, 22–24, 34, 67–75, 78–79, 84–85, 88–94, 98, 110, 134–135
African American English (AAE) tradition. *See also* Shoptalk in classroom; Shoptalk in hair salon
  characteristic features, 74–75, 140–141
  community-based language, 7–8
  cultural border crossings, 36, 67–85, 110–114
  dialogically structured argumentation, 37–42
  empowering identities, 80–84
  Jali in, 90–91, 133–135
  learning to cross borders, 110–114
  linguistic and paralinguistic features, 16, 39, 41, 71, 74–75, 77, 134, 140–141
  reading dialect, 91
  shifting landscape and response to change in Chicago, 109–110
Agre, P., 34, 44
Alvarez, A., 80
American Educational Research Association, 120n1
Angela (hair salon apprentice), 45–48, 50–53
Angelou, Maya, 112
Ansari, S., 114, 150
Anyon, J., 34, 80
Anzaldua, G., 10
Apprenticing

  in classrooms, 118, 120–122, 123–124
  in hair salons, 45–48, 50–58, 60–66, 101, 106–107, 123
  in product orientation (Rogoff), 28–29
  rigged scripts, 60–66, 101
Arnett, J. J., 29
Au, K., 5, 148

Bakhtin, Mikhail M., 40, 71, 80, 84
Banks, J. A., 18, 103–104, 108, 119
Baquedano-Lopez, P., 29
Barley, S. R., 44–45
Barton, D., 1, 16
Bell, Derrick A., 17, 39–40
Bennett, William, 126–131
  comments as basis of metacognitive instructional conversation, 128–131
  curriculum design approaches based on comments, 133–147
  radio show comments, 126–128
Berliner, P., 140
Black public spaces, 13–15, 24–27
Black Public Sphere Collective, 14
Booth, W. C., 36
Border crossing
  African American discourse, 13–15, 24–26, 36, 37–42, 67–87, 89–94, 110–114
  apprenticing in classrooms, 118, 120–122, 123–124
  apprenticing in hair salons, 45–48, 50–58, 60–66, 106–107, 123
  Black public spaces and, 13–15, 24–26

Problem solving, *continued*
135–139
  empowerment through social reading
    orientation, 107–108, 150–151
  rigged scripts in hair salons, 60–66,
    101
  socialization through Shoptalk,
    94–102
  social reading of narrative texts,
    72–75, 129–131, 135–139
  strategies for, 20
Process orientation (Rogoff), 27–28,
  34, 105–106
Product orientation (Rogoff), 28–29,
  34, 106–107

Rabinowitz, P., 33, 36, 151
Racial socialization, 29, 113–114
Rahla (novice hair stylist), 61–62, 66,
  106–107
Reagan, Ronald, 129
Repertoires of practice, 50–60, 64–66,
  102–103
Republican National Committee, 117
Resnick, D., 1
Resnick, L., 1
Rigged scripts in hair salons, 60–66,
  101
Rivera, A., 29
Rogoff, B., 4, 25–29, 35, 37, 47, 52,
  66, 84, 88–89, 103, 105, 107, 108,
  145
Rose, Mike, 28, 34
Rosenblatt, L., 149, 151
Rotherman, M. J., 29
Rymes, B., 48, 52, 64

Sasse, D., 104
Schank, R. C., 28, 48
Schultz, K., 16, 60
Scribner, S., 1, 4, 14, 44, 53, 65
Shoptalk in classroom, 116–147
  apprenticing, 118, 120–122, 123–124
  border crossing by language minority
    children, 85–87, 110–114
  challenges of analyzing, 12–13
  color-blind discourse, 14–15, 17–18,
    110, 114

critical consciousness, 103–104
culturally aware and relevant
  instruction, 13, 17–18, 66
culturally responsive teaching and
  learning, 13
Cultural Modeling framework (Lee),
  12–13, 119–121, 124–126, 128,
  132
curriculum design, 118–122, 132–
  147
deficit perspective, 13, 118, 149–151
dialogically structured
  argumentation, 131
discourse communities, 121–122,
  124–131
dualism regarding norms of talk,
  144–145
ethnography of, 20–21, 30–31
guided participation, 118, 132–147,
  149
I-R-E (Initiate, Respond, Evaluate)
  participation structure *versus*, 134,
  138
learning to cross borders, 110–114
narratives of understanding, 15–17
overview of Shoptalk process, 11
participatory appropriation, 118
as pedagogical (teaching) instrument,
  25, 115
repertoires of practice in home *versus*
  school, 65–66
risk discourse, 114–115, 118–119
separation between home and school
  cultures, 66
Shoptalk, defined, 12, 24
strategies of inquiry (Hillocks), 121,
  122–123, 125
texts of the everyday, 124–147
traditional narrative approach
  compared with, 13–15, 120–122,
  134, 138
transformative equity-based
  framework, 17–21, 103–104
Shoptalk in hair salon, 1–5
  as activity system, 24–27
  apprenticing, 45–48, 50–58, 60–66,
    106–107, 123
  assumptions concerning, 26–27

About the Author

Yolanda J. Majors is an associate professor, writer, and dedicated wife and mother. She lives in Minnesota, where she is the associate director of Adolescent Literacy and Learning of the Minnesota Center for Reading Research, University of Minnesota.